Walking th̲ ̲.̲.̲.̲.̲.̲.̲.̲.̲.̲.̲
of Sussex

David Bathurst

Photographs by David Bathurst

S.B. Publications

By the same author:

The Selsey Tram
Six Of The Best
The Jennings Companion
Financial Penalties
Around Chichester In Old Photographs
Here's A Pretty Mess!
Magisterial Lore
The Beaten Track(republished as The Big Walks Of Great Britain)
Poetic Justice
That's My Girl
Walking The Coastline Of Sussex
Best Sussex Walks
Let's Take It From The Top
Walking The Disused Railways Of Sussex
Once More From The Top
Sussex Top Tens
Walking The Kent Coast From End To End

Contributions to:
Introduction to *While I Remember* - autobiography of Anthony Buckeridge
The Encyclopaedia of Boys' School Stories

To my father, Peter

First published in 2008 by S.B. Publications
14 Bishopstone Road, Seaford, East Sussex
Tel: 01323 893498   Email: sbpublications@tiscali.co.uk

ISBN 978-185770-3375

Designed and Typeset by EH Graphics, East Sussex (01273) 515527

CONTENTS

Front Cover: *The river Arun at Arundel on a golden autumn day.*

Title Page: *The Greatham Bridge crossing of the river Arun.*

Back Cover: *Rural idyll - one of the picturesque lakes beside which Christians River flows,
complete with beautiful lakeside house.*

ABOUT THE AUTHOR

David Bathurst was born in 1959 and has enjoyed writing and walking throughout his adult life. He has walked all of the principal long-distance footpaths of Great Britain including the Pennine Way, West Highland Way, South West Coast Path, Offa's Dyke Path and the Coast To Coast Walk; he has also walked the entire coastlines of Sussex and Kent, and his guides to these walks were published by SB Publications in 2002 and 2007 respectively. By profession David is a solicitor and legal adviser to magistrates in Chichester and Worthing. He is married to Susan and has a daughter, Jennifer. When not writing or walking he loves cycling, the works of Gilbert & Sullivan and Flanders & Swann, vintage TV sitcom, teashops, and the Times Deadly Killer Sudoku. His most notable achievements have been the recital of the four Gospels from memory on a single day in July 1998 and the recital of the complete works of Gilbert & Sullivan from memory over 4 days in August 2007.

AUTHOR'S ACKNOWLEDGMENTS

I would like to thank Lindsay Woods of SB Publications for her encouragement and support, Liz Howe for her tremendous work in putting the book together, and my wife Susan and daughter Jennifer for their constant love and understanding.

SELECT BIBLIOGRAPHY

Buildings Of England - Sussex, by Ian Nairn and Nikolaus Pevsner - Penguin 1965
The Companion Guide to Kent And Sussex, by Keith Spence - Companion Guides 1999
Walking The Disused Railways Of Sussex, by David Bathurst - SB Publications 2004

INTRODUCTION

The Sussex landscape is endlessly fascinating for the walker, with so many contrasts, from sprawling coastal settlements to remote farmland, from large urban modern developments to quiet country towns, from magnificent chalk downlands to quiet meadows. Among the most timeless features of the landscape are the rivers and streams that run through the county. Some, like the Arun, Adur and Ouse, have played an important part in the economic life of the community, providing a means of transporting goods and materials, and even today, Shoreham Harbour at the mouth of the Adur and Newhaven Harbour at the mouth of the Ouse are two of the busiest ports in south-east England; many of the rivers of Sussex have been used as a source of water for such purposes as irrigation, sheep washing and the powering of mills, and at least one river has provided sand and reeds for thatching; fishing has been, and remains, an important pursuit along large stretches of the rivers; and some have been used for leisure purposes, especially the Arun with its many pleasure boats, although many more have provided a refreshing swim on a hot day, and the faster flowing and/or narrower sections have offered excellent opportunities for canoeing or keenly-fought games of Poohsticks! Some of the rivers have had a very considerable impact on their surroundings, such as in January 1994 when the bursting of the banks of the river Lavant caused serious flooding around Chichester, and in the autumn of 2000 when the overflow of the rivers Uck and Ouse following weeks of heavy rains caused devastation to the communities through which they flowed.

Arguably the best way to appreciate these rivers, with their own individual character and variety historical or topographical interest along their banks, is on foot. As a riverside explorer of Sussex you'll not only meet rivers of tremendously varying size and surroundings, but you'll get to know a good deal more about Sussex itself. You'll encounter major urban centres, pass round or through delightful small towns and beautiful villages, meet intriguing man-made features such as castles, landscaped gardens, disused railway lines and ancient churches, and enjoy the beautiful surrounding countryside, with magnificent South Downs and Wealden scenery, dramatic seascapes and rolling pastures as well as some unsung beauty spots which are well off the beaten tourist track, and a rich diversity of wildlife and plant life. Moreover, you'll find riverside walking in itself to be a very therapeutic exercise. Rivers are timeless and dynamic, reminding us of changeless things in a world that seems to change sometimes too fast for our own good, and a "walk by the river" has been and will continue to be acknowledged as a relaxing, pleasurable and invigorating experience.

The purpose of this book of described walks is to provide the foot passenger and armchair traveller with a description of a ramble beside each of the rivers of Sussex. A glance at a map will show that within East and West Sussex there are a formidable number of watercourses including streams, brooks and inlets. To describe a route beside each one would be an impossible task, and this book is therefore restricted to those watercourses that are named on modern large scale OS maps as rivers. All "named" rivers that flow through Sussex for at least some of their length are included, with the exception of

North River, a tributary of the Arun which is all but inaccessible to walkers, and the Teise, which follows a small part of the Sussex/Kent border but flows through Kent for virtually all the remainder of its length, only a derisory section encroaching into Sussex. Where a river does flow into or from another county, generally only the section of river that flows through Sussex is described. The rivers are of varying length, and the extent to which one can stick to the riversides themselves also varies from river to river. The Adur, for instance, can be followed for its entire length from the point at which its western and eastern arms meet, whilst the banks of almost all of the Kird are privately owned and inaccessible, with limited opportunities for glimpses of this pretty stream in the heart of the Sussex countryside. Some of the walks, such as the Mole, are reasonably short and can easily be completed in half a day, but others, such as the Ouse and the East Sussex Rother, will need two or more days to accomplish, and you'll need to decide whether to tackle them in day trips or to seek accommodation on or close to the route. Some walks combine two rivers in one: for instance, it is logical to take the Line and the Brede in one go, and Christians River and the Cuckmere River together. Some lend themselves to being done as detours off a bigger river walk, for instance the Limden as a detour from the East Sussex Rother, and the Uck from the Ouse.

I aim in each case to describe a continuous walk which follows as close to the river being described as possible, and follows as much of the river as possible while still incorporating features of interest that are close by. Some walks are able to pick up a particular river at source and follow it all the way to its end, but others may pick up the river some way downstream of its source. It is often very hard to tell where a named river actually does "start" and a look at an OS map or atlas will show in the case of some rivers a number of tributary streams which then join to form the river in question. Infant rivers are much more prone than wider rivers or estuaries to flow through private land with no public access and no possibility of a continuous and rewarding walk along the bank for its early miles at least. The Ouse is a good example of this. Moreover, I have deliberately aimed to start and finish each walk at places that are reasonably well served by public transport; not everyone has access to a car, and using public transport not only permits far greater flexibility but is much less damaging to the environment.

As far as possible, the described routes follow established rights of way. There are, however, sections of route which are not designated rights of way, and this fact is made clear in the relevant parts of the text. I have endeavoured to apply a common-sense approach and eschew stretches of riverside where e.g. padlocked gates, fencing or "keep out" signs make it clear that visitors are not welcome, or where to stick to the river would require negotiation of terrain which is unreasonably demanding on the average walker. However that still leaves a number of stretches where access is possible but debatable, e.g. gates secured by easily unknotted ropes, or low wooden fencing that can easily be stepped over. When in doubt as to whether to follow a section of route which is stated in this book not to be a designated right of way, especially if to access it requires the surmounting of a man-made obstacle (however small), it's best to seek permission from the relevant landowner; the local public library should be able to assist you if you are unsure as to who owns the land in question. Landowners may in fact be only too pleased to allow considerate walkers access to their land. If you decide to walk along a stretch that isn't a designated right of way without permission, you do so at your own risk. Whether you've permission or not, and this goes for any of your riverside walking, you MUST observe the basic rules of the countryside, avoid damaging private property, especially crops, and leave things exactly as you found them. And of course you should NEVER trespass onto live railway lines. I recommend that you carry with you the local Explorer map in case it becomes impossible to follow a section of described route that isn't along a designated right of way, although such occasions should be rare.

Most of the walking will be extremely easy, the main potential problems being mud or excessive undergrowth. During spells of wet weather, riverbanks can become squelchy and often slippery, with a profusion of long wet grass, and in such conditions you would be well advised to wear overtrousers or gaiters to prevent your trouser legs getting either sodden, or filthy, or both. Walking boots aren't necessary, and indeed for the shorter walks you may find it more comfortable to walk in trainers or stout shoes. On some of the longer walks, amenities can be quite sparse in places, so bring supplies of food and drink. You should drink lots of water on hot days, not waiting until you are thirsty, so carry plenty of water with you; I have learnt the hard way that you should never EVER be tempted to drink from the rivers themselves, nor indeed the tributary streams that feed them. The walks never take you too far from civilisation but if you are reliant on public transport you need to check bus and train times in advance, noting that bus services are often nonexistent on Sundays. I have indicated in the text routes on which Sunday buses did not operate at the time of writing; it should be assumed that, where there is no Sunday service, there will be no Bank Holiday service either. It is therefore best to have numbers of local taxi firms handy!

Happy walking.

David Bathurst
February 2008

A Note about the Maps

Please note that the maps prefacing each walk description are not to a uniform scale. The grey line on each map depicts the course of the walking route, not the course of the river itself.

LOCATION OF WALKS

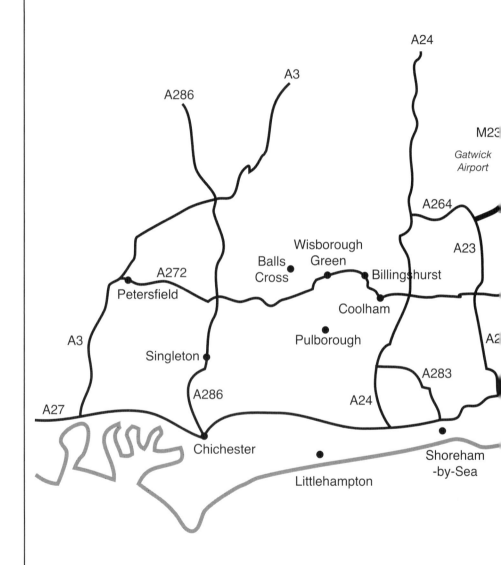

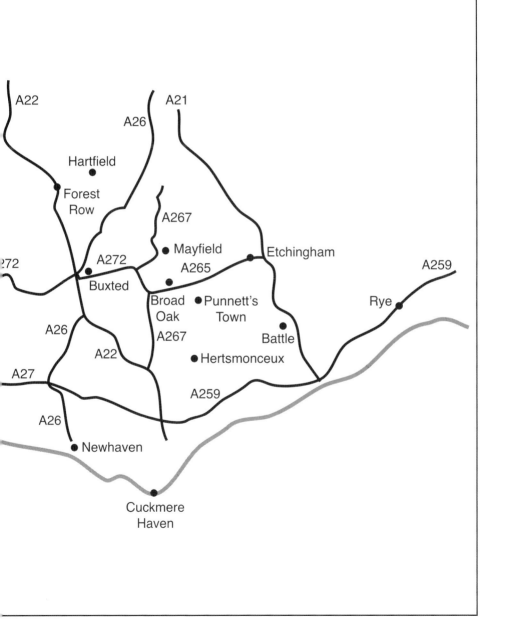

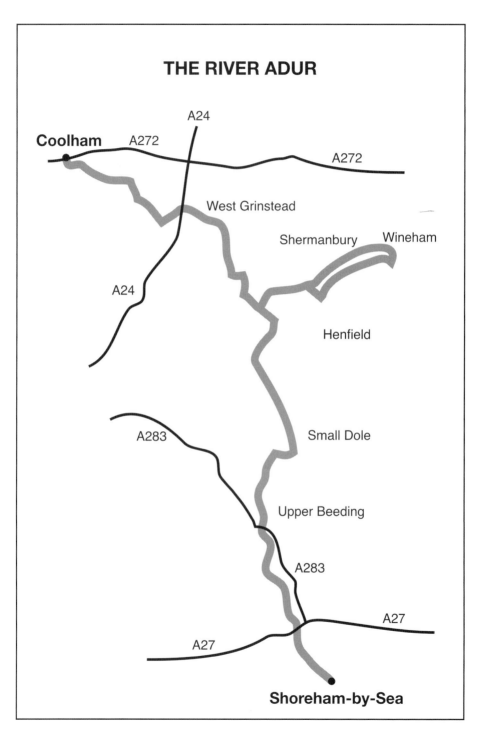

THE RIVER ADUR

A24

Coolham   A272

A272

West Grinstead

Shermanbury   Wineham

A24

Henfield

A283   Small Dole

Upper Beeding

A283

A27

A27

Shoreham-by-Sea

THE RIVER ADUR

Length:	Approximately 20 miles depending on start point.
Start:	Coolham (western arm) or A281 at Bull Inn by Mock Bridge (eastern arm).
Finish:	Shoreham-by-Sea.
Public transport:	Regular although infrequent buses from Horsham to Coolham (not Sun); regular buses from Horsham to Brighton serving Partridge Green, A281 and Henfield; regular buses from Shoreham to Worthing and Brighton; regular trains from Shoreham to Worthing, Chichester, Brighton, Haywards Heath and London.
Refreshments:	Pub at Coolham; shops and pubs at Partridge Green; shops, pubs and cafes at Henfield (slightly off route); shops, pubs and cafes at Steyning (off route); shops and pubs at Bramber; shops, pubs and cafes at Shoreham.
Conditions:	The first part of this walk provides a choice, with two arms of the Adur as far as Betley Bridge, from which it's possible to follow the river all the way to its mouth at Shoreham along excellent paths.

Following the river: The Adur (locally pronounced "Aider") is one of the major rivers of Sussex, its valley forming an important gap in the chalk hills of the South Downs. For a long time it enjoyed extensive commercial usage for virtually all of its length; it effectively serviced the shipbuilding industry at its mouth at Shoreham, with boatloads of timber from the Weald being conveyed along the river to the port. At one time it was known as Bramber Water and got its present name in the 16th century to reflect the supposition that the Roman town of Portus Adurni was built on or close to where Shoreham stands now. It's unique in West Sussex as having two distinct "arms" for its upper reaches, but once both arms come together the walking is both straightforward and very satisfying, with a riverside path available for the whole of the rest of the route. The two "arms" provide two possible options for you as you plan your walk along the Adur, and each option is described below.

The western arm begins in the centre of Coolham, an attractive village close to its source. Walk southwards along the B2139 but shortly turn left onto a signed bridleway.

Follow the bridleway past the very attractive pond at St Julians, then keep on the obvious path just south of east over the site of a World War Two airfield, going straight ahead at a signed bridleway junction. Cross a road and follow the bridleway beyond, soon veering left to cross the infant Adur and then right to reach a road. Turn right onto it, soon passing Shipley Windmill, one of the finest in Sussex; built in 1879, it was once owned by the author Hilaire Belloc. Just before the road bends sharp left, you turn right onto a signed path, passing just to the right of the fine 12th century Shipley Church. Go forward to the river, then bear left to follow the left bank, soon reaching a footbridge which you cross. Proceed as signed past the Church Farm South building, joining a track taking you to a road; turn left and follow the road, going straight on at the road junction and continuing south-eastwards past two footpath turnings to the left. Cross a wide tributary of the Adur, then rise slightly and in a few hundred yards beyond the tributary crossing turn left onto a signed footpath. The path, which is not very clear on the ground, descends through a field to a footbridge over the Adur; beyond the footbridge the path, heading north-east, becomes much clearer and arrives at a T-junction with the Knepp Castle estate road. Bear right to follow this road and soon you will pass the ruin of the original Knepp Castle which is to your right. The ruin consists of a fragment of a Norman keep that was built by the Braose family, probably in the 11the century as a subsidiary of Bramber Castle. Continue along the estate road to arrive at the A24.

Cross the A24, taking great care. Almost immediately opposite on the other side is a footpath heading just south of east; take this path which descends through a field, crosses a tributary stream and turns sharp right, then shortly turns left and rises, following a right-hand field edge. Soon you see West Grinstead Parish Church in front of you, and

Looking across the river Adur to Lancing College Chapel.

12

you simply head for the church, following the signed path to enter the churchyard and pass immediately to the left of the front door of the church. The church is dominated by its 13th century tower, and inside there's a part 11th century nave, some fragments of wall painting and some large monuments. The backs of the pews in the church are unusual in that local farm names have been inscribed upon them. Just beyond the church, turn right at the T-junction of paths and descend to be reunited with the Adur; don't cross the footbridge, but just before it turn left onto a path which now follows the left bank of the river for roughly two miles. This is a lovely path, with the Adur beside you throughout, and you can enjoy excellent views to both the surrounding meadows and indeed on a clear day towards Chanctonbury Ring on the South Downs. As you proceed, the ground underfoot does tend to get juicier and in places, after heavy rain, the going could be quite challenging. You pass a very attractive weir, and for the first time you get the feeling of quite a substantial waterway; all the same, it is hard to believe that at one time this stretch of river would have seen considerable traffic, including the Knights Templar on their way downstream by barge from their estate at Shipley. A few hundred yards after the weir there's a footbridge just beyond which a footpath sign directs you off to the left, away from the river. However there is nothing to prevent your proceeding all the way to Lock Bridge, where the Adur meets a metalled lane, and although this isn't a designated right of way, you should have no difficulty in walking it. Otherwise, you'll need to follow the signed footpath away from the Adur. This is very clearly defined, proceeding initially immediately to the right of a line of trees then through a more open landscape, gaining a little height as it continues. You turn sharply left and pass to the western side of some farm buildings to arrive at a T-junction of footpaths, at which you turn right, going forward to a clear track. This proceeds eastwards, crossing the Downs Link (about which more below) and arrives at a T-junction with the B2135 in the village of Partridge Green. Turn right onto the B2135 and follow it; the main centre of the village can be reached by taking the next turning on the left immediately beyond the pub, but to get back to Lock Bridge you need to follow the B2135 over the old railway bridge and then take the signed footpath, actually a metalled lane, leading off to the right almost immediately beyond the bridge. It's then a walk of almost a mile along this lane to get to Lock Bridge. The advantage of this much longer route is that you get to visit Partridge Green which although unremarkable in architectural terms has a good variety of shops as well as the opportunity for liquid refreshment!

Beyond Lock Bridge, you're temporarily forced away from the Adur. Head eastwards along the lane (if you took the longer route via Partridge Green, you will therefore have a bit of backtracking to do) and in a few hundred yards bear right along a signed path heading firstly just east of south then just west of south, aiming for Pinlands Farm. Follow the signs carefully through the fields, arriving at a T-junction with a track just short of the farm, bearing right onto the track, swinging left towards the farm then going left as directed past the farm buildings. Beyond the farm you can see the Adur in front of you;

follow the signed path southwards then swing eastwards to gain the bank. Now enjoy a delightful walk along the left bank as far as Bines Bridge on the B2135. Sadly, just as you were beginning to get into your stride, you must again lose the river at Bines Bridge, although from here virtually the whole of the rest of this western arm of the Adur is visible. Bear left onto the B2135 then almost immediately turn right onto a signed path that snakes uphill round the left side of the buildings of Bines Farm, then swings in a nor'north-easterly direction along a right-hand field edge, arriving at a T-junction with a track. Turn right onto the track then almost immediately left, as signposted, to pass the buildings of Brightmans Farm. Again, beyond the farm buildings, swing just north of east and descend along a left-hand field edge; just before the field boundary at the bottom, turn right along a signed path eastwards and climb the embankment to turn right onto the Downs Link footpath. Follow the Downs Link and in half a mile you will arrive at Betley Bridge where the Downs Link meets the eastern arm of the Adur close to its confluence with the western arm. Cross Betley Bridge and immediately turn right onto the left bank of the river to begin your continuous riverside walk to the sea.

The starting point of a walk beside Adur's eastern arm is the Bull Inn which is just a short distance beyond Mock Bridge on the A281 two miles north of Henfield; there's a convenient bus stop on the Horsham-Brighton route outside the pub, and the pub itself offers convenient refreshment at the end of a circular walk round this part of the Adur. To begin your walk, make your way from the pub back across Mock Bridge, almost immediately turning right onto the Shermanbury Estate road. The road proceeds most pleasantly through parkland, allowing limited views to the Adur which lies to your right, and in fact becomes separated from the Adur by the little church at Shermanbury, situated on a hill above the estate road. The church contains medieval walls, box pews, a curly timber chancel arch and a font that dates back to around 1300, and there's also a timber bell turret. The road returns to within sight of the river and passes two footbridges, the second an impressive raised footbridge by a weir; beyond the footbridges, the road loses the Adur, narrowing to become a path and proceeding through woodland, arriving at a T-junction with the metalled Fryland Lane. Turn right into the lane and follow it, soon passing a secluded cemetery with a chapel, and emerging from the woods into serene meadows. The Adur becomes visible again to your right. Continue along the lane to a T-junction with Wineham Lane at the south end of the hamlet of Wineham, turn right into Wineham Lane and very soon arrive at a bridge over the Adur. This is not the source of the Adur, but it is the furthest east that its course can be traced by the walker. It rises a little further east, being fed by various tributary streams that emanate from the vicinities of Burgess Hill and Hurstpierpoint.

From Wineham Lane you will now be working your way back to the A281, but you will be on the other side of the Adur and within sight of the river virtually throughout. Cross the bridge and look out for a gate and grassy slipway on the right (west) side of Wineham Lane; proceed through the gate and go down the slipway to arrive in the meadows on the south side of the Adur, making your way to the bank of the river. Now proceed beside the Adur, heading in a westerly direction. The first half mile or so of the bank walk is not a designated right of way, and although at the time of writing there was no difficulty of access the position may change in future, and you may think it prudent to seek permission to walk this section if you are in doubt. If access becomes impossible you will need to follow Wineham Lane southwards for another quarter of a mile, turning right on to a public footpath that proceeds westwards to Abbeylands Farm then swings just west of north to arrive at the bank. From here on, you can enjoy a very pleasant walk indeed through quite delightful scenery, the Adur itself fairly narrow but offering

A swan's eye view of the Adur and the railway crossing near Shoreham.

tremendous variety with waterfalls contributing to the beauty of the river hereabouts. When you reach the raised footbridge over the weir which you passed when following the Shermanbury Estate road, you will see a footpath sign with arms pointing right and left. You need to take the left path here, away from the Adur; it squeezes between thick bushes on one side and an electric fence on the other, and uses a footbridge to cross a tributary stream. After rain the stream is quite turbulent at this point and the narrow footbridge crossing is a bit of an adventure! Beyond the footbridge continue along the path just west of south with the buildings of Shiprods Farm to your left. As you pass the buildings you arrive at a path junction with a signed footpath pointing to your right; turn right onto this path, keeping an area of vegetation to your left, and follow the left-hand field edge, proceeding south-westwards on a straight course. This is lovely open walking on a reasonably well-defined path with great views down to the Adur. Eschewing a path which heads off to the right and goes over the Adur to form a link with the Shermanbury estate road, and also ignoring a path heading left to Nymans Farm, continue south-westwards, heading unerringly for the A281. You can see the attractive arches of Mock Bridge to the right, and watch the Adur disappear beneath this busy road. Proceed to the A281, here concluding the circular walk encompassing the eastern arm of the Adur, for The Bull Inn is straight ahead of you on the other side of the road.

Reaching Betley Bridge from Mock Bridge can be achieved in one of two ways. It may be possible to follow the right bank, which you gain by following the A281 from the Bull Inn across Mock Bridge, bearing left through a gate immediately beyond the bridge, and then joining the bank. However, it is not a designated public right of way: it may be obstructed and you should seek permission from the owners before attempting it. If you're able to walk it, you will enjoy a good straightforward walk to Betley Bridge, and a taste of the bank walking that will provide easy riverside progress all the way on from Betley Bridge to Shoreham. If you decide not to walk it, or are precluded from doing so, walk up the A281 briefly north-westwards from the river, bearing left onto a track that takes you past a jumble of buildings to Fairacre. The track swings left and peters out. Bear right here onto a path which heads south-westwards across two fields and through a line of trees, crossing a stile then continuing just south of west over a further field to cross a tributary stream. Now veering a little north of west you continue through open pastures, passing just to the left of an attractive lake, to arrive at the Downs Link. You're now united with the western arm route. Turn left onto the Downs Link path and follow it to Betley Bridge as described above.

When you reach Betley Bridge and join the left bank, you can now relax and start enjoying the Adur properly with no more route-finding problems. The walking from Betley Bridge is initially exceedingly peaceful, and you are hardly aware of the sprawl of Henfield which lies not far away to your left. You soon pass a picturesque weir, just beyond which is the confluence of the eastern and western arms of the Adur, and you continue in a south-westerly direction through an unspoilt pastoral landscape. Now you begin to swing south-eastwards, passing Bineham Bridge; the landscape to your left, separating you from the western fringes of Henfield, is an amazingly intricate network of narrow streams across flat fields. In the meantime, the Downs Link, which follows the defunct Shoreham to Christ's Hospital railway, has been going south-westwards from Henfield, and shortly you meet it again, rising to cross over it. The bridge to the right, now a footbridge, was once a crossing of the Adur on the old railway line, but nowadays any danger is likely to come from Downs Link cyclists! The Downs Link is open to bicycle users as well as walkers and riders, so look carefully as you cross over and then regain the bank of the Adur beyond. Just to your left, beyond the crossing, is the part-timbered and part tile-hung Streatham Manor, the original main manor house of Henfield. Continue along the bank, heading just east of south; this is unremarkable but peaceful walking and there is a sense of timelessness about your immediate surroundings. The Adur now swings in a more westerly direction, and as you follow the bank round to the west with the river, you will see the buildings of Steyning to your right, while the magnificent Lancing College Chapel can be observed towering above the meadows beyond. Keep going through the meadows, enjoying superb views to the South Downs escarpment to your left; this particular section of the Downs includes not only Truleigh Hill, the mast of which you can clearly see on the hilltop, but the perennially popular

Devil's Dyke. The Adur swings in a more southerly direction again, snaking just west then just east of south, with Upper Beeding now becoming apparent to your left and the twin settlements of Bramber and Steyning across the Adur to your right. At length you arrive at a crossing of the Bramber-Upper Beeding road.

Before proceeding beside the Adur towards the sea, you may wish to detour to visit Bramber and Steyning, reached by turning right on to the road and walking westwards. Bramber boasts a castle ruin, the original building dating back to the 11th century, a Norman church, and a fine timber-framed house called St Mary's which was built in the 15th century. As stated above, the Adur was once known as Bramber Water, in recognition of the fact that ships once routinely sailed upstream from the sea to Bramber and Steyning, and it was only when the estuary silted up that a port had to be built nearer the mouth of the river. Steyning, reached by proceeding on to the roundabout junction with the A283 and continuing as signposted from the roundabout, is a beautiful town with a quite magnificent late Norman parish church and numerous fine town houses, the best of which are to be seen in the High Street and Church Street. Returning to the Adur and continuing along the left bank beyond the Bramber-Upper Beeding road, you'll have noticed a subtle change in your surroundings. Not only have the quiet meadows been replaced by areas of housing, but the peace and serenity that have been a constant feature of your walk from Betley Bridge towards Bramber are now rather overtaken by the noise of traffic from the very busy A283 and A281 which meet close to the river hereabouts. Indeed, it is only a short riverside walk from the Bramber-Upper Beeding road to the A283 itself, which crosses the Adur and the riverside path by means of a rather inelegant modern bridge. Beyond the bridge, the surroundings become dominated by the busy A283 as it proceeds towards the sea, and, worse still, the derelict Upper Beeding cement works. As you approach the works, you come to a footbridge which carries the South Downs Way over the Adur and enables you to switch to the right bank as far as Old Shoreham Bridge should you wish to do so. The advantage of switching to the right bank is that you will be able to visit two fine ecclesiastical buildings that lie close to the river, namely St Botolph's Church and Lancing College Chapel.

If you decide to stick to the left bank, the walking remains easy but unremarkable. For a short while beyond the footbridge there is an overlap between your riverbank path and the Downs Link as it briefly forsakes the old Shoreham to Christ's Hospital railway line. As you pass the cement works, the Downs Link path is seen to go off to the left, resuming its acquaintance with the course of the old railway, but you should continue on the riverside path. The walk from here to the A27 overbridge crossing is straightforward and enjoyable, particularly if you're able to come to terms with the ever-present traffic noise from the nearby A283. The twists and turns of the Adur make this a longer walk than the Downs Link, with which it in due course becomes parallel, but the going is very simple and the views across the river to the nineteenth century Lancing College Chapel get better all the time. It is a landscape of real contrasts, with the chapel and surrounding downland providing a majestic backcloth to the flat river valley while the overbridge and spaghetti-like A283/A27 junction get ever closer. Whatever you may think of modern road building, this is a magnificent feat of engineering and you may well feel some admiration for those who designed and constructed it as you pass beneath the huge concrete supports. Once you are beyond the overbridge you can clearly see the buildings of Shoreham and its airport ahead of you, while you will observe that the Downs Link, reunited now with the course of the old railway, is immediately beside you and to your left. About a quarter of a mile south of the overbridge you reach Old Shoreham Bridge where the right bank detour described below comes to an end. You could make a short detour here to the nearby church of St Nicholas just over the other side of the A283; the church is a fine old building with many Norman features.

If you choose to follow the right bank as far as Old Shoreham Bridge, cross the footbridge just before the cement works and join the bank on the other side. However, once over the bridge you may wish to turn right and follow the bank briefly upstream, then turn left with the South Downs Way and soon left onto the road to reach the church of St Botolph in the hamlet of Botolphs. The church is wonderfully unspoilt, containing some late Saxon features and a splendid Jacobean pulpit. Return now to the bank and follow the right bank downstream; immediately to your right are flat fields but beyond them is a rolling downland landscape with the ground rising to over 400 feet. Lancing College Chapel now dominates the view immediately ahead, and an opportunity to detour to this great building arises about two miles beyond the footbridge, when the right bank path leaves the Adur briefly to follow beside a tributary channel and then meets the metalled Coombes Road at Cuckoo Corner. To make the detour, turn left onto the road at Cuckoo Corner and follow it for about half a mile, then bear right onto the chapel approach road, simply following it round to the chapel itself. Begun in 1868, the chapel was built in early 14th century English Gothic style using Sussex sandstone and its foundations are in places seventy feet deep. Return to Cuckoo Corner, and follow the path along the south side of the tributary channel, soon regaining the right bank of the Adur. Continue along it, soon passing underneath the A27, then following a narrow stonier path sandwiched between the river and some industrial works which are protected by some formidable fencing. Immediately beyond the works, and just short of the airfield adjoining Shoreham Airport, you reach the footbridge known as Old Shoreham Bridge. Turn left and cross over the bridge to regain the left bank. Just at the point where the alternative paths unite, you can make the very short detour across the A283 to visit the church of St Nicholas, Old Shoreham(see above).

As you proceed along the left bank from Old Shoreham Bridge, you will notice how the surroundings have become more urban.You have the choice between walking by the water's edge or the Downs Link which provides perhaps firmer going without sacrificing the views. However in due course the Downs Link gives out, and when it does so it's necessary to drop down to the waterside to continue. Initially the going, effectively along the beach beside the river, is unpromising, but very shortly you're able to climb up to an embankment path which proceeds to the railway bridge. The railway crossing isn't aesthetically the most pleasing construction but it is a vital one, carrying trains on the very busy Brighton to Worthing line. You pass under the bridge to join a concrete riverside walkway past new housing developments which lie to the left, and continue along this walkway, passing not only the apartments but some inventive sculpture work, all the way to the A259 road bridge crossing. Slight anticlimax follows; you can't follow the Adur for the short distance to its mouth at Shoreham Harbour, so instead turn left and follow the road straight on into Shoreham's main street. In due course, beyond the shops on the right, you will find yourself walking beside Shoreham Harbour, with its impressive assembly of vessels and harbourside apartments. Shoreham, which became established as a port in Norman times when silting of the Adur estuary made it less easy to navigate, is a cheerful, bustling town with ample shops and cafes. Its two most interesting buildings are the church of St Mary de Haura (literally, "of the harbour") which dates back to 1130 and boasts particularly fine choirstalls and a very prominent tower, and the Marlipins, a very rare example of a surviving secular non-military Norman building of distinctive chequerboard flint. Shoreham was one of the leading ports of the medieval period, exporting a huge variety of goods, and was also renowned for its shipbuilding; a further development which boosted the port's fortunes was the laying of oyster beds within the river mouth, bringing prosperity to fishermen and carriers who made daily journeys to the capital with the freshly caught delicacies. Ideally placed to serve the rapidly developing towns of Brighton and Hove, it continued to thrive as a most important port and by the end of the 20th century it was handling 3 million tonnes of cargo per year. Having enjoyed refreshment in the town, you can reach the station from the waterfront by going up Church Street, turning right at the end into St Mary's Road, and then left at the T-junction into the busy Brunswick Road. The station is a short way up Brunswick Road on the right-hand side.

Journey's end - the Adur arrives at Shoreham Harbour.

THE RIVERS ARUN, CHILT & STOR - MAP 1

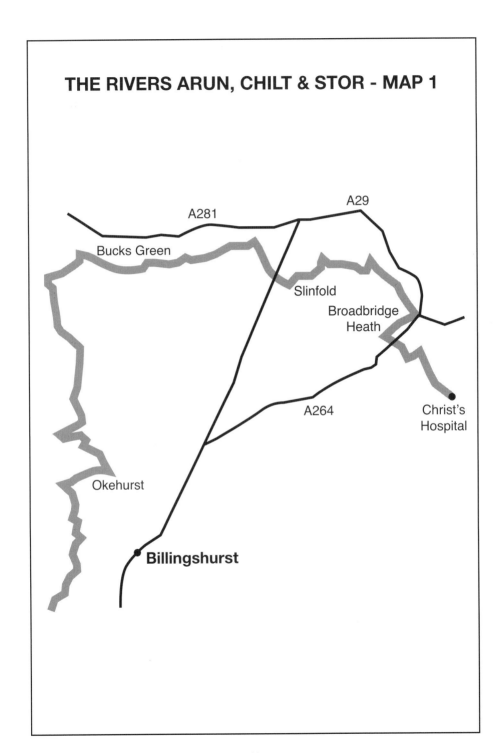

THE RIVERS ARUN, CHILT & STOR

Length:	Approximately 30 miles. (8 further miles for Chilt/Stor detour)
Start:	Christ's Hospital.
Finish:	Littlehampton.
Public transport:	Regular trains along the Arun Valley line, serving Chichester, Arundel, Amberley Pulborough, Billingshurst, Christ's Hospital and Horsham; regular buses linking Rudgwick with Horsham and Guildford (not Sundays); regular buses linking Pulborough with Midhurst, Petworth, Storrington and Worthing; regular buses linking Arundel with Worthing; regular buses linking Littlehampton with Worthing, Brighton, Chichester and Portsmouth; regular trains linking Littlehampton with Worthing, Bognor Regis and Barnham with connections for Chichester and Portsmouth.
Refreshments:	Pub and shops at Rudgwick; pub on Loxwood Road; pub and shop at Wisborough Green (off route); shops, pubs and cafes at Billingshurst (off route); pub at Stopham Bridge; pubs, shops and cafes at Pulborough; café at Wiggonholt; (Chilt/Stor walk: pubs, shops and cafes at Storrington;) pub and shop at Amberley; café at Houghton Bridge; pub at Offham; pubs, shops and cafes at Arundel; pubs, shops and cafes at Littlehampton.
Conditions:	As far as Bury there is only limited riverside walking but the countryside is delightfully unspoilt with many fascinating features. From Bury onwards the river walk is almost continuous and provides the finest riverside walking in West Sussex.

Following the river: Most people, when asked what images they associate with the Arun, will think in terms of the impressive band of water that meanders majestically past the magnificent castle and other historic buildings of Arundel. The Arun, however, has its origins considerably further north. It rises in the vicinity of Horsham and twists and turns for many miles, initially in the Horsham suburbs and then striking out into the beautiful unspoilt countryside midway between the North and South Downs. Although even in its early stretches it stands out among its many tributary streams and brooks, it is only around Pulborough that it becomes a truly impressive waterway, and it's only from a point just downstream of Pulborough that it is navigable for rivercraft.

It's not realistically possible to follow the course of the Arun for its opening miles in the vicinity of Horsham. Some stretches may be walkable, but they aren't on designated rights of way and the presence of obstructions will mean much frustrating backtracking. The walk described below starts at Christ's Hospital station, close to the famous Christ's Hospital school, a grand redbrick construction dating back to 1902. The school is of much older origin, and as you alight at the station you may see some of the students with their distinctive uniform of long blue topcoat, white neckbands and yellow socks. From the station forecourt, follow the approach road then soon turn left along a signed footpath, initially metalled then grassy, past the right-hand end of a row of houses. The signed track bends left (ignore the stile on this bend) and passes underneath the railway, then proceeds through woodland, along a field edge and then through another small wooded area, to arrive at the Arun. You can now enjoy a riverside walk of about half a mile, keeping the river to your right, initially walking in the shade of trees then emerging into the meadows. The Arun at this point, though quite active especially after wet weather, is still in its infancy, and presents a huge contrast to its estuarine waters near its mouth at Littlehampton over 30 miles away. It is lovely walking so early on in your

The pretty church at Wiggonholt, where the detour from the Arun
to follow the Stor and the Chilt begins.

journey, and it's a shame that on arrival at a T-junction of paths you're forced away from the river.

Turn left at the T-junction and follow a wide track for a couple of hundred yards, ignoring the first (unsigned) field path between fences but then shortly turning right onto a signed footpath along a right-hand field edge, aiming for the buildings of Wellcross Grange. You are then signposted round the left side of the Grange, keeping an aircraft landing strip immediately to your left, and indeed you should watch out for light aircraft both on the ground and airborne! Go forward to arrive at the main A264 road, cross the road with care and turn right, then follow the A264 for half a mile or so to the roundabout junction with the A281. About halfway along, you cross the Arun again but sadly there's no chance of access onto the bank, and so you must continue to the roundabout. On arrival at the roundabout, bear left to follow beside the A281(first exit) briefly, then very shortly bear left onto a metalled lane signposted "footpath." You swing slightly left (north-westwards), passing a complex of buildings to your right, and go forward to a pleasant assembly of buildings where the metalled lane swings left. At this point you leave the lane, heading very briefly right (north), crossing a bridge over a small stream. Turn immediately right onto a signed path, going parallel with the stream, then very soon turn right over another bridge and from there bear immediately left, slightly west of north. Keeping the stream to your left you walk through the open field, then go forward into another field, heading steeply uphill, aiming for the Rapkyns Farm complex. At the top of the hill follow the signposts carefully, bearing left then almost immediately right to pass round the left side of a hilltop pond. Pause to enjoy the views back to the Arun valley before proceeding, as sight of it will be very limited for the next few miles. Bear left again to walk briefly parallel with the Rapkyns approach road, then, faithful to the signpost, veer shortly right to join the approach road; you turn left on to it, the buildings of Rapkyns just ahead of you, but then almost immediately bear right onto a narrower path. This proceeds fractionally west of north then swings left to arrive at Cook's Lane onto which you turn left, then follow the lane just west of south through the trees. In 300 yards or so you reach a signed path entering a field. Follow the path diagonally through the field in a north-westerly direction, aiming for the left corner of a wooded area, then, carefully observing the footpath direction signs, veer a little left, just north of west, to arrive at the Nowhurst Farm buildings. Follow the footpath signs carefully through the farm complex, arriving at a T-junction with a bridleway.

Turn left onto the bridleway, again heading just north of west, ignoring a path going off to the right. Shortly the bridleway turns sharply left, steeply downhill, then right, along a left-hand field edge. *Incidentally, over to your right is a tributary of the Arun called North River, but there's no real chance of either accessing or walking beside it for any of its length.* You soon arrive at a footpath junction; take the left path and immediately you find yourself reunited with the Arun, which you keep just to your right as you head first south-westwards then westwards, with a hillside and hilltop Rowfold Farm immediately to your left. Your path enters woodland and ascends, and as you climb you can enjoy a lovely view to the Arun valley down to your right, in a gorgeous setting amongst trees and meadows. This is one of the highlights of the section between Christ's Hospital and Rudgwick, and it's a shame when your path, having risen through the trees, loses sight of the Arun. You arrive at the approach to Hill House and now turn sharp left onto a metalled lane that goes steadily downhill, south-westwards. However, in a couple of hundred yards you need to look out for a signed path leaving the lane to the right; follow this path through fields in a north-westerly direction to arrive at the A281, cross the road and turn right, then almost immediately bear left onto a signed bridleway which takes you to the hamlet of Dedisham. This is a lovely walk, with the Arun valley immediately before you. You pass the old Dedisham School building, going forward to Dedisham Manor and swinging left with the lane, shortly thereafter arriving at a signed path which forks off to the right. Take this fork which leads you down through a field to a junction with another lane; you turn left (southwards) here, but just in front of you to the right is a footbridge crossing of the Arun and a good opportunity to view the river. Having done so, you proceed briefly southwards along the lane, but very soon turn right and now head just south of west along a clear path to Violets Farm, with lovely views of the Arun all the while to your right. You pass some fine woodland to your right – the sight of the Arun flowing through or round this is particularly pleasant – and soon arrive at the buildings of Violets Farm including the stunning timber-framed main farmhouse. Contrary to what is shown on some OS maps, the signs (ignore one going off hard left here) clearly direct you westwards round the left side of the farm, and you're then signed sharp right then left to get you back onto the westerly course shown by the map.

As signed, you head westwards then just south of west, aiming for a stile in a large area of fenced woodland directly ahead of you. Proceed over the stile, going down to cross a small but active stream by a plank bridge, then, continuing in the same direction, go forward to arrive at the embankment of the old Horsham-Guildford railway. Not only are you on the course of the old line but also on the Downs Link footpath, which you will have encountered on your walk beside the River Adur and which overlaps with the old railway for much of its journey. Climb steeply onto the embankment and turn right; very shortly a signed path* goes off to the left and you need to take this path, but by walking a couple of hundred yards further on you reach a bridge over the Arun. It looks exceedingly picturesque seen from above, and there's a signed viewpoint available here, although sadly there is no riverside walk. Half a mile further up the Downs Link path you reach the village of Rudgwick with a shop, pub and bus connections to Horsham and Guildford, and as there are no other easily accessible amenities for many miles beyond, this may be a detour that's worth taking. If you do, you'll need to return to the asterisked path above. Follow this path, fractionally south of west, steeply down the embankment and along a right-hand field boundary heading roughly westwards, then at the corner of the field go forward into the next field as signposted, again keeping the boundary to your right. The Arun is visible through the vegetation to your right. The path rises slightly and bends a little to the right, but is clearly defined and soon reaches a T-junction with a wider path. Turn right here and proceed along this wider path, then take a signed and clearly defined footpath shortly leading off to the left, with fences on each side, and the Arun visible down to your right. You arrive at a T-junction with a lane onto which you turn right, immediately reaching a T-junction with a road onto which you turn right, but then you almost at once bear left onto a signed footpath.

Proceed along the footpath that goes down to arrive at the Arun, cross it by means of a footbridge and go forward to enter a large field. Although it's not totally clear on the ground, you need to aim for the left-hand field edge and proceed to the exit at the top left-hand corner of the field, coming out at Loxwood Road onto which you turn left. Some easy road walking now follows, and there's the added bonus of a roadside pub, the Mucky Duck, the only on-path refreshment opportunity between the start of the route and Stopham. Continue past a right-hand turn shortly beyond which are nurseries on the left, and it's just past the nurseries that you bear left along a signed path, keeping a tall hedge to your left. Continue along this path in a dead straight line, then after a few hundred yards turn right onto a signed path that goes off at right-angles. This very pleasant path begins in the shade of woodland but soon swings sharply left, and you emerge into open fields looking ahead to a wind pump towering above the surrounding trees. Initially you keep a field boundary fence immediately to your right, but a signpost soon directs you into the adjacent field to your right, and you now proceed along the left-hand edge of this field, passing to the right of the wind pump. Very soon after this you will see the Arun again on your left-hand side, and you now have a very enjoyable field walk keeping the Arun to your left.

The Greatham Bridge crossing of the river Arun.

Continue beside the Arun, heading towards an area of woodland, but before you reach it a signpost directs you left to one of the most picturesque parts of this section of your walk. You go over a footbridge across a weir, then bear right round the right-hand edge of what looks like a private garden to arrive at a lovely assembly of buildings including an old water mill and a delectable timber-framed cottage. At the T-junction with the track turn left, then take the signed path that leads off almost immediately to the right, keeping the Arun to your right. The Arun is now lost to sight for a while as you proceed initially through a field then into attractive woodland, emerging and rising slightly to cross another field; although it's disappointing to have temporarily lost the river, there are at least good views to the Arun valley to your right. Shortly you reach a farm road and now have a choice of routes to Bignor Farm. You could go straight over the road and proceed through the fields as directed by the signposts, but you should be warned that bulls graze in these fields. A more prudent course may be to turn left up the farm road; at the end turn right onto the minor road then shortly right again onto a wide track that brings you to another minor road. Turn right and follow this road until you reach Bignor Farm.

At the farm buildings, look out for and join a signed footpath leading off to the right; the first part of the path seems to encroach into a front garden, but soon you find yourself in another field. You now descend quite steeply, aiming for a stile on the other side, and follow the signed route to arrive once more at the Arun. Don't cross the footbridge but proceed along the left bank; sadly your meeting with the river is a brief one, for all too soon the signpost points you away from the river in an easterly direction, back to the road onto which you turn right. [If you are in a hurry you could simply follow the road to this point from Bignor Farm.] Now follow the road for the best part of a mile until you arrive at the farm buildings at Okehurst on the right-hand side, then just before you reach the buildings turn right onto a track that snakes round the edge of the buildings and subsequently heads back towards the Arun. Follow the signed path until you arrive back at the river. You actually walk parallel with the river upstream briefly, then cross the footbridge to arrive at a junction of paths; this is a key moment on your walk, for you are now able to join the Wey South Path, which you will keep to more or less all the way to Pulborough with consequently little or no route-finding difficulty. Turn left onto this path and follow it southwards, keeping the Arun to your left, while to your right is the course of the Wey & Arun Junction Canal which opened in 1816 and remained operational until 1871. The canal is gradually being restored to its former glory, with some fine stretches of water and restored locks and bridges, although at the time of writing there were also many dry sections and rather dilapidated and neglected pieces of canal engineering. The Wey South Path was opened in 1975, and although it is not one of the "heavyweight" long-distance paths in the South of England, the Path's guidebook alone has sold over 10,000 copies. Now continue along the Wey South Path, which from its raised platform provides fine views of the course of the nearby Arun, to reach the A272 crossing at Newbridge. Refreshments are available in Wisborough

THE RIVERS ARUN, CHILT & STOR - MAP 2

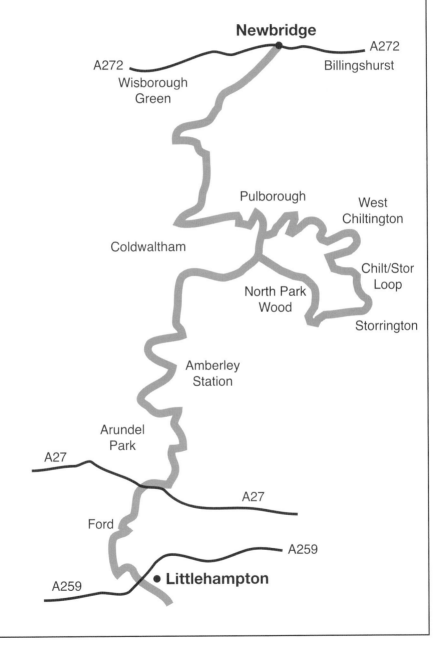

Newbridge

A272
Billingshurst

A272

Wisborough
Green

Pulborough

West
Chiltington

Coldwaltham

Chilt/Stor
Loop

North Park
Wood

Storrington

Amberley
Station

Arundel
Park

A27

A27

Ford

A259

A259

● Littlehampton

Green, a mile and a half to the west, while a mile and a half to the east is Billingshurst, which offers a rather wider range of amenities and regular train services.

Cross straight over the A272 and follow the Wey South Path southwards, soon swinging south-westwards. Initially the Arun is immediately beside you to your left, but then the river bends away to the left while the path continues in a more or less straight line, keeping the canal immediately to the right. South of Newbridge, the canal when operational was known as the "Arun Navigation" and lasted a few years longer than the Wey & Arun Junction Canal. The river swings back to meet the path and in fact at this point you switch banks, using a footbridge across the river to make further progress. Sticking to the Wey South Path, you now continue beside the canal, passing Lording's Lock which has recently enjoyed extensive restoration, and soon afterwards arrive at a seating area beside a splendidly restored brick-built footbridge over the canal. Cross the bridge then continue beside the canal which is now to your left, the Arun still in view to the right. Just to the east of Shipbourne Farm, and with a large barn immediately to your left, you reach a prominent footbridge over the Arun; at this point you turn left on to a path that goes over the canal and follows round to the right of the barn. Still on the Wey South Path, bear right onto a path that proceeds through open fields in a south-westerly direction and drops down to cross first the canal, then the Arun. Continue along the path, rising slightly, to the point where the signed path turns 90 degrees to the right.

Follow the signed Wey South Path westwards, going forward to arrive at a metalled

The verdant banks of the Arun between Greatham and Bury,

driveway with a house directly ahead of you; the Wey South Path, which you continue to follow, crosses over the driveway to the right of the house, and now proceeds uphill. As you rise, you will note the ground falling steeply away to your right, creating a very picturesque effect indeed. Continue along the clearly defined path, going forward towards the trees, and proceed in the same direction along a path through a strip of woodland, with open fields beyond the woods on each side. You emerge at a metalled road, and turn left to follow this road for about half a mile, past Westland with its amusing sign warning you to beware of low flying owls! The road starts to climb – you will pass a sign advising of a steep gradient – and as you proceed quite steeply uphill (but before reaching a sharp left hand bend; if you get to this, you've gone too far) look out for and join a signed path with the distinctive Wey South Path logo going off to the left through the woods. It is in fact more of a track than a path, with a good firm surface. After just over a quarter of a mile it bends sharply left, then on reaching the edge of the woods swings to the right and drops down to the Arun. Ahead of you is a fine view of the Toat monument, a castellated hilltop tower rising some 40ft high and constructed in 1827 as a memorial to Samuel Drinkeld who four years previously had died as a result of a fall from his horse. As you descend, there are also lovely views to the Arun upstream, so you can at least follow with your eyes what you will not have been able to follow with your legs! In due course you arrive back at the river bank and bear right.

Continue from here southwards along the Wey South Path, but then, staying with the Wey South Path, you very shortly bear left to cross the Arun, turn right and after a pleasant wander through the meadow climb to join a wider track slightly further east of the river, parting company from the Arun. Unfortunately you won't see it again for a good two miles. Follow the track as it continues southwards, bending sharply westwards, to arrive at a road at the hamlet of Pickhurst. Turn right onto the road and follow it for about a mile and a half; it's not enthralling walking and after a long day's tramping you won't appreciate its winding and undulating course. Finally at a sharp left-hand bend, look out for the Wey South Path signpost pointing you off the road up a track to the right. Follow this quite steeply uphill, turn right at the top of the hill towards the wooded area, and then bear left onto a path that proceeds along the top edge of the woods, still sticking to the Wey South Path. Soon you are rewarded for your tarmac crunching and climbing by a magnificent view through the trees to the Arun below; this is a quite delightful walk, with tremendous views not only to the Arun but the South Downs escarpment which has now opened up in front of you and which will be in your sights for many miles to come. You now begin to lose height, and drop gradually to arrive at the busy A283 beside the very modern road bridge over the Arun. Cross the A283 carefully and take the signed footpath, surely one of the shortest signed public footpaths in the country, arriving in just a few yards at the old Stopham Bridge over the Arun, and the White Hart pub, with its quite beautiful riverside setting.

Having enjoyed bridge and pub, turn left onto the old road – now effectively superseded by the A283 – and follow it to arrive at the A283 a little way east of the new Arun crossing. You must now endure a disagreeable eastward walk of just under a mile beside this very busy road with no pavement, the only saving grace being the view to the right including the Arun close to the roadside. Fortunately as you approach the railway bridge on the outskirts of Pulborough a pavement starts, and you follow the pavement beside the A283 to the roundabout junction with the A29 coming in from the right. There's a useful tearoom a little way down the A29 just before the bridge, and beyond is the bridge itself where the A29 crosses the Arun. Frustratingly the bank on both sides is closed off to the public, so having enjoyed the view from the bridge return to the roundabout and continue briefly eastwards to the next roundabout where the A29 goes off to the left. Staying with the A283, continue in the same direction into the centre of Pulborough which is about half a mile distant, as far as the old post office which is on the left. Pulborough is an attractive village with a long street and a fine 13th century church which boasts an impressive tower; the Arun has always been a significant focal point in the village, and the Pulborough eel was regarded as a tasty local delicacy! Opposite the old post office, turn right down a path that descends to the river and bear left to walk along the bank. It's good to be back on the riverbank, enjoying a taste of proper riverside walking with the promise of much more to come between here and Littlehampton. Cross a footbridge at the confluence of the Arun with the Stor, and continue forward till you reach a footpath sign pointing to the left, away from the river. The river bank ahead is blocked by a no entry sign, and between here and Greatham Bridge you're again forced away from the river and will need to take the signed path as shown. Follow the marked path across the meadows to a gate then continue as signposted, bearing slightly right and proceeding in a straight line across the next field, dipping gently downhill. Then, again as indicated by the signpost, turn left and proceed to a gate leading to a track that goes quite steeply uphill to the beautiful little church at Wiggonholt which dates back as far as the 13th century. Although you have left the river bank, the views across the Arun valley are quite delightful.

From Wiggonholt you can embark on a circular walk beside sections of the Stor, a tributary of the Arun, and the Chilt which flows into the Stor. To do so, follow the church approach road eastwards to the A283, then turn right to follow alongside this road, passing a road going off to the right and then taking the signed track a little further along to the left. The track curves gently left then bends very sharply right, and it is just past this right bend and a little way short of Redford House that you turn left onto a path that goes steeply uphill. As you emerge from the trees, turn hard left and follow the field edge all the way round, soon finding yourself within sight of the attractive little river Stor to your left. Keeping the river to your left, and walking upstream, descend to Hurston Lane, a narrow metalled road. Your way is to the right, but it's well worth detouring slightly left to reach the bridge over the Stor, which is quite delightfully situated. Now retrace your steps and proceed along the road up the hill, enjoying views down to the Stor upstream of the Hurston Lane bridge crossing.

At the sharp right-hand bend in the road, do not bend right with it but take the signed footpath off the road, following roughly the direction in which you've just been travelling, and now proceed through attractive woodland. Emerging from the wood and passing through a gate, you descend briefly and are treated to a beautiful view towards the South Downs escarpment. Descend to the fence then turn left as directed by the signpost, and go forward across a stile; ahead of you in the valley you now see a sewage works and, aiming roughly for the works, you follow the footpath as directed, with an area of fairly thick vegetation soon apparent to your left. The walking is now very straightforward as you continue along the left-hand edge of Parham Airfield (watch out for low-flying gliders) while to your left is woodland and a pleasant stream which is a tributary of the Stor, although at least one map of this area describes this tributary as the Stor itself! The sewage works are just across the river but once you have left them behind the surroundings become more rural and unspoilt, and although the tributary stream is hidden in the trees for the most part, there are many occasions on which it can be seen and enjoyed. Soon a signpost directs you into the wood and you find yourself walking beside the stream which you shortly cross by means of a simple footbridge. Continue beside the stream, soon reaching a footpath junction; take the footpath leading off to the right, and follow it briefly downhill, aided by wooden steps, to the river, which you cross by means of another very basic footbridge. Keeping the river to your left, you now continue along the path and go forward to enter a caravan park, following the tarmac drive through the park. Beyond the park you keep along the driveway to come to another footpath junction, now approaching the village of Cootham. Go straight on to the A283 to arrive at a crossroads; your route is directly over the crossroads into Chapel Lane but you may decide to detour to the left to visit the popular Crown Inn.

Follow Chapel Lane, a short but most attractive little street with one old cottage that boasts a date plaque. The road bends right then sharp left, and as you reach the left bend there's a really splendid view to the South Downs between Amberley and Washington. I walked this section on a miserable afternoon in late November and was treated to a remarkable sight of a low bank of cloud, like a giant strip of cotton wool, hanging over the top of the escarpment. Beyond the left bend Chapel Lane ends and you go forward to a clear path that proceeds resolutely through a broad expanse of pasture, and goes forward and downhill to a footbridge over the stream. From the footbridge, proceed along the path, going forward to arrive at New Town Road; cross straight over this road onto another footpath that brings you back to the B2139. Cross the road and bear left towards the centre of Storrington, but soon turn right into Fern Road which you follow, heading for a monastery on the left-hand side of the road. Immediately before the monastery, turn left onto a signed public footpath, and follow this path, aiming for the part-11th century parish church of Storrington and its churchyard. The path passes through the churchyard to the left of the church and drops down to Church Street, arguably the most picturesque street in the village. Turn left onto the street but almost immediately turn right into Brown's Lane, going forward into Meadowside where you will meet the Stor again. Just after crossing over the river the road negotiates a hairpin bend to the right of which is a children's play area, and it is here that you can detour to view the source of the Stor. To do so, pass through the play area, exit through the gate at the far end, bear left up the path to the road, turn right onto the road then take the next left turn and bear almost immediately right on to a footpath which goes steeply uphill. A lake, where the Stor begins, can be seen to your right. After pausing to enjoy the

The river Arun at Arundel on a golden autumn day.

surroundings, including the South Downs escarpment which is very close by, retrace your steps to the hairpin bend on Meadowside.

From the hairpin bend it's now possible to walk down to the riverside and follow the bank of the Stor through a sort of mini-country park, this grassy area providing an oasis of greenery amidst the modern housing development. Soon you reach an information board and a footbridge river crossing; go over the footbridge then bear right, going forward to a residential area and, keeping the Stor to your right, proceed to Storrington's bustling main street. Storrington does have two notable associations: it was the inspiration for the fictional village of Tillingfold in Hugh de Selincourt's novel *The Cricket Match*, and the composer Arnold Bax spent the last years of his life in the village. Interestingly, the river Stor derives its name from the village rather than the other way round. Cross straight over the road and proceed along Old Mill Drive, noting the Stor on your left as it reappears from under the main road. Soon you approach a duckpond, into which the Stor flows, across a grassy area to your left, and here you join the footpath that leaves Old Mill Drive and proceeds round the right hand side of the pond. Continue round the pond in an anti-clockwise direction, towards a bridge carrying the path over the Stor as it flows away from the pond. Do not cross the bridge but just short of it turn right through a wooden gateway and drop down to enjoy a lovely walk which takes you initially along the right bank of the Stor on a good path, then over the Stor and along the left bank. Shortly you reach a T-junction of paths; don't turn right over the footbridge, but turn left on to a path which leads up to the residential Spierbridge Road. Turn right into this road and almost immediately right again into Fryern Close. Follow the close round, and as it bends for the second time back towards Spierbridge Road, turn right onto a footpath which proceeds slightly west of north.

This is an enjoyable walk on another good path, with the Stor and unspoilt countryside to your right, and modern housing development to your left. A signpost then directs you right, across *a footbridge over the Stor and down some steep steps. The path continues uphill through attractive woodland, soon reaching a T-junction with a lane that has a very tranquil rural feel, and it is hard to believe that you left the busy village centre just minutes ago. The lane swings gently to the right and reaches a T-junction with a lane on to which you turn left, soon crossing the Stor once more. Continue up the lane to a T-junction with Hurston Lane and follow this lane north-westwards to yet another bridge crossing over the Stor. Climb quite steeply from the bridge, and where at the top of the hill Hurston Lane does a 90 degree turn to the left, you continue straight on along a signed path past Hurston Street Farm. Ignoring a footpath going off to the right, continue forward on what becomes a grassy and possibly muddy path going downhill, with woodland ahead of you. The ground levels out, and you proceed to a T-junction with a driveway onto which you turn right, then walk briefly north-eastwards to the meeting point of two metalled roads, Heather Lane and Sunset Lane, at the extreme south-west corner of the sprawling village of West Chiltington Common.*

Turn right and follow Sunset Lane eastwards. Although this isn't an enthralling road walk, there is at least variety in the architecture of the houses, and the vegetation surrounding them is diverse and attractive. Continue along Sunset Lane beyond the crossroads with Westward Lane, at length arriving at a T-junction with Monkmead Lane; turn right along Monkmead Lane but very shortly turn hard left into Common Hill and follow it north-westwards past the houses of West Chiltington Common. In roughly a quarter of a mile, turn left onto a signed footpath opposite the point where Fir Tree Lane goes off to the right. You are now about to make your acquaintance with the river Chilt for the first time and you can detour a short way beyond the footpath turn to a bridge over the river; although the source of the river is further east, there are no stretches of riverside walking available upstream of this point. Now proceed along the signed footpath opposite Fir Tree Lane heading fractionally south of west in a straight line. Soon the path bends sharply to the right and then left, and you enjoy a delightful walk in the shade of trees, the babbling Chilt immediately beside you and to the right. You arrive back at Monkmead Lane onto which you turn right, shortly crossing a bridge over the Chilt, then just beyond the bridge turn left onto a path which again proceeds parallel with and to the right of the little river. Continue along the path, soon reaching a much wider path at which you will become aware of Pulborough Golf Course to your left. Turn right onto the path, and soon arrive back at Monkmead Lane on to which you turn left.

Between here and Wickford Bridge, a good two miles away, the Chilt is out of sight and almost completely inaccessible. Follow the road north-westwards past impressively large residential properties, continuing north-westwards at the next road junction, then shortly beyond the junction take a signed footpath going off to the left. This in fact goes parallel with, then over, a delightful little stream, and reaches the Chilt at the edge of the woods across the fields. Unfortunately you cannot join the river bank here so enjoy what you can see of the Chilt, both upstream to your left and downstream to your right, and then pause on the bridge over the Chilt to enjoy the beautiful unspoilt surroundings. Now continue into the woods and after crossing another footbridge climb steeply to a gate; pass through the gate and, taking great care, cross two fairways of the golf course you met earlier, the fairways interspersed by a narrow pathway through intervening heather. Follow the signposts carefully, and don't stray from the designated path route across the fairways, rather aiming for the gate across the other side of them, passing through it and continuing along the path. Now descend to Golf Club Lane, the metalled drive linking the golf club with the A283; turn right onto the drive and follow it to a T-junction with the A283, turning right to follow alongside this busy road.

Your walk beside the main road is undeniably one of the less enjoyable sections of your journey, although there is a grass verge available for much of it, and you have the Stor for company immediately to your right; you can follow this as far as Wickford Bridge, just before which is its confluence with the Chilt. It's not immediately possible to gain the bank of the Stor going westwards from Wickford Bridge but you get a good view of the river as it proceeds, extensive thick vegetation draping both banks. From Wickford Bridge follow the A283 north-westwards towards Pulborough, thankfully soon reaching a parallel pavement, along which you continue by the roadside past the pub and small parking area. A couple of hundred yards beyond the pub,

look out for a signed footpath going away to the left, and take this path to arrive shortly at the river bank; although it is a narrow channel of water, it was still flowing well during my visit on a hot August afternoon. You are now able to follow the embankment that runs parallel with the river on its north side, enjoying not only the spectacle of the river but the beautiful valley scenery around you and the South Downs escarpment in the distance. Although on two occasions you need to scramble down the bank to get round barbed wire fences, there is no difficulty in keeping to the riverside all the way to its confluence with the river Arun; this is a delightful spot and blissfully off the beaten tourist track. Having reached the Arun, you can return to Wiggonholt by following the Arun walk described above.

Back at Wiggonholt, you

Arundel's sloping High Street, a magnet for tourists and a natural stop-off for those walking the banks of the river Arun.

continue with your Arun walk by proceeding to the small car park area and church signboard, adjacent to which you will see a stile with a footpath leading southwards from it. From the stile, follow the footpath which initially descends, then gently climbs to reach the car park of the visitor centre for the Pulborough Brooks nature reserve. It is worth detouring to the centre, which not only offers superb views across the Arun valley but provides a wide range of information about the wildlife to be found in the reserve. The footpath arrives at a T-junction of paths immediately beyond the car park; turn right here, keeping the car park and visitor centre to your right, and having enjoyed the fine view descend through the thick woodland. Shortly you reach another T-junction of paths, and keeping a fence immediately to your right, turn right and continue through the woods. You ascend gently, and the path swings to the left to arrive at the road linking the A283 with Coldwaltham; turn right onto the road and follow it for the best part of two miles. For tarmac crunching, this is actually quite agreeable walking on what is a very quiet road which passes the delightful hamlet of Greatham with its tiny 12th century church, immaculately kept churchyard and manor house with 17th century features. At length you reach a bridge crossing of the Arun, known as Greatham Bridge. Just before the bridge you turn left onto a signed path and initially follow the riverbank, but sadly you're forced away from the riverside, ascending gently along the path to reach a T-junction with a sandy track. Turn right onto this track and follow it past a house and chicken run, just past which you bear sharp left, keeping a high hedge on your left-hand side. Proceed along the track, following the signposting which directs you sharply right and downhill, then bear sharp left just beyond the house at the foot of the hill, before shortly turning right again immediately beyond a fence into an area of lush grass punctuated by marsh plants. The path, which is here rather indistinct on the ground, doesn't proceed exactly parallel with the fence but goes at a slight angle to it, aiming for a footbridge. The surroundings hereabouts are absolutely delightful; although you are some way from the Arun itself, you are now back in the Arun valley with constantly improving views to the majestic South Downs escarpment.

Cross the footbridge and continue, heading in a virtually straight line for Amberley. Although the path is now better defined again once over the bridge, the going underfoot can be extremely squelchy in or after wet weather, and deteriorates further as you reach a T-junction with a wider track. Turn right at this junction and follow the track which in a few hundred yards leaves the valley floor and climbs briefly to a T-junction with a road. When you arrive at the road, turn right and go forward to the junction with Amberley's main street. Turn right onto this street, a delightful mixture of thatch, tile, timber, flint, brick and stone, and follow it past the village pottery and Norman church. Close by is Amberley Castle, a square-towered construction dating back to the 1370's to defend the upper reaches of the Arun valley. It never saw military action and became a summer retreat for bishops, its moment of glory perhaps coming in October 1651 when it's believed that Charles II stayed here in the course of his flight to France following the Battle of Worcester. The road peters out and becomes a public footpath, initially metalled but continuing as a dirt track; keep on the track to the railway, crossing with great care, then continue as signposted across the fields. In good weather, the view from here to the spire of Bury church across the river, with a backcloth of the South Downs escarpment, is stunning. At length you arrive at the river bank, and from now on you will have the Arun beside you virtually all the way to the sea. Turn left to follow the bank, soon reaching an impressive footbridge which the South Downs Way, the national trail linking Winchester and Eastbourne, uses to cross the Arun. Here you can switch banks as there's now a footpath along both, although it matters little which bank you use as both paths bring you to the next road junction. If you switched banks by means of the bridge, you could also detour back upstream to view the beautiful village of Bury, boasting a most attractive church built of Downland materials with a shingle spire and 12th century features, and a number of impressive houses including

the Tudor-style Bury House where the author John Galsworthy lived. At one time, there was a useful ferry crossing over the Arun at Bury. You then need to backtrack to the South Downs Way footbridge.

Whichever bank you choose to progress downstream from this footbridge, continue beside the river to arrive at the B2139 at Houghton Bridge, and its tempting tea gardens immediately adjacent. It was here that Charles II crossed the Arun during his escape to France. Cross straight over the B2139 and resume your riverbank walk using the right bank; this is a particularly attractive section of the Arun, the lush pastures and woodland of the valley set against the steep banks of the nearby Downs and the wooded hills forming part of Arundel Park. You cross a couple of minor streams by plank bridges

Arundel Castle, one of the most striking sights to be observed from the banks of the river Arun.

– these could be slippery in wet weather, so be careful – and proceed in the shade of trees, soon reaching a T-junction with a bridleway. Turn left and follow the bridleway into the woods bordering Arundel Park, keeping the river close by to the left and a wall to your right and in due course passing (but not going through) a metalled kissing gate in the wall. For now, you find yourself away from the river bank and the walk temporarily loses the feel of being a true riverside promenade. Continue on the bridleway; the path twists and turns through an area of woodland, climbs to emerge from the wood at a stile, proceeds along a field edge downhill, and swings right and left into another wooded area. Climb again and emerge, the track now wide and following another field edge. The gaps in the trees to the left do permit good views to the Arun.

You're now approaching the village of South Stoke; you pass some farm buildings then bear right beyond a flint wall, the track proceeding parallel with the wall to a metalled road. Turn left onto the road, then soon take a left fork that begins as a metalled road but soon becomes a track which passes by the 11th century St Leonard's Church with a medieval tower. Continue along the track to just short of a bridge over the Arun, and here turn right onto the riverside path, keeping the river to your left. This is a super walk along a good clear path with the Arun beside you, the South Downs rising up behind it to the left, and Arundel Park continuing to dominate the scene to your right; shortly you will see Arundel Castle towering up above the trees. You reach the hamlet of Offham and pass the Black Rabbit pub, proceeding through the metalled courtyard, and go forward to the road. Turn left onto the road but very soon, just opposite the Coach House, turn left onto another riverside path which you can now follow all the way to the centre of Arundel. It's lovely walking, with superb views ahead to Arundel. To your right, shortly after you pick up the path again at the Coach House, are the lakes and ponds of the Arundel Wildlife and Wetland Trust, with its fine collection of ducks, geese, swans and many migratory birds. Across the river to the left you can see the Arun Valley railway line, and as you continue towards Arundel the peace of the surrounding landscape will be disturbed by the noise of the nearby A27. In due course you arrive in Arundel and the path comes up to meet the road just short of a junction with the town's main street, which in turn crosses the Arun by means of the bridge immediately adjacent. Proceed over the main street to the little quayside, then follow the road round to the right to arrive at the town square. Arundel is a natural stopping place on your journey, with its wealth of beautiful buildings, interesting shops and many places offering refreshment. The town developed as a result of its situation at the river crossing on the major East-West route through Sussex, and at one time it was a port, handling such goods as wine from France and coal from Newcastle. Its chief glory is its castle which although it looks ancient was in fact rebuilt in the 18th century; all that remains of its original fortification is the 12th century shell keep and fragments of the 13th century barbican and shell wall. Arundel also boasts a Gothic-style 19th century cathedral and a 14th century parish church, but if you are into creature comforts or retail therapy rather than history, both the High Street and Tarrant Street house large numbers of cafes, pubs, restaurants and specialist shops. It is along Tarrant Street – the first left turn off the town square looking up the hill – that you must proceed to continue your walk. Follow Tarrant Street to the far end, then bear left along a walkway that brings you down to the riverside again. Proceed along the riverside path and under the bridge carrying the A27, then continue along the path beside the river out of Arundel. Your walking is now very easy, proceeding downstream along the right bank of the Arun on a very well-defined embankment path. In contrast to the dramatic downland vistas of the preceding miles, there is a certain grandeur and nobility in the flat, sweeping landscape around you, and the views back to Arundel and its cathedral and castle are a constant delight. After heavy rainfall many of the nearby fields are prone to flooding and this can actually enhance the beauty of the surroundings. You pass close to Ford, previously an important junction on the county's once flourishing canal system and now best known for its open prison. Two and a half miles of walking bring you to the A259 bridge crossing of the Arun, where it's necessary to climb away from the river and cross the road, but another path more or less directly opposite brings you back to the river bank, and suddenly you find yourself propelled into a much more urban landscape. Although you're again briefly separated from the river by fencing, and need to take care to follow the signed path, you soon find yourself back beside the river, and can now proceed confidently towards Littlehampton Marina with a variety of rivercraft in evidence immediately to your left. Think back to the Arun around Christ's Hospital and Rudgwick where the river was barely wide enough to accommodate a bath-tub, let alone a pleasure cruiser! Continuing to follow the signposting, you're then forced away from the river to arrive at the road linking the A259 with the swing bridge, which is now immediately to your left. Littlehampton, standing at the mouth of the Arun, is just across the bridge.

Cross the bridge, enjoying a grandstand view of the marina, and when you reach the other side turn immediately right into River Road. Proceed along this road, which has a somewhat hemmed-in feel thanks to modern housing development to your right and left, then shortly enter and follow an alleyway leading off to your right, which takes you to a waterfront walkway past the new housing. You can now enjoy a splendid waterside walk, firstly along the new paved area, then along the side of Pier Road, and forward to a promenade to East Pier where the Arun finally flows majestically into the English Channel. It is a splendid climax to your Arunside walk, and you may want to pause as you arrive at East Pier and reflect on a journey of constant joys, surprises and contrasts. To access the centre of Littlehampton, retrace your steps to Pier Road and continue along Pier Road until you reach the modern shopping precinct. Littlehampton, which really came to life in the 19th century, certainly lacks the charisma of Arundel but remains a pleasant and bustling town, being both a popular family resort and a busy workaday place with an extremely active harbour and distinguished shipbuilding history. It was an important port in Saxon times, and in the Middle Ages was a landing place for Caen stone from Normandy which was used in churches and secular buildings throughout Sussex. During both world wars, Littlehampton became an important military base, and the town has expanded radically since, with considerable residential and industrial development; although its importance as a port has declined, it is today a popular resort and base for pleasure cruises up the Arun, fishing and the dredging of marine aggregates. To reach the station, bear left into the High Street and keep going forward into Terminus Road, where you will find the station to your right.

THE RIVER EMS

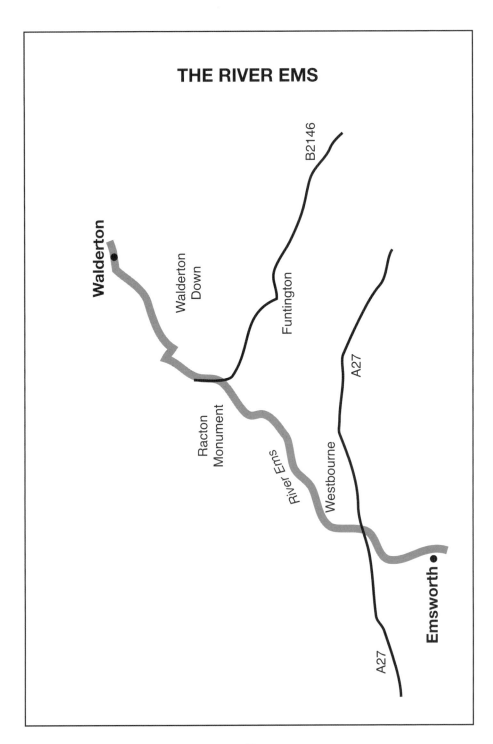

THE RIVER EMS

Length:	6 miles.
Start:	Walderton.
Finish:	Emsworth.
Public transport:	Regular buses to Walderton on the Chichester to Petersfield route (not Sundays); excellent bus and train services from Emsworth to Chichester and Portsmouth.
Refreshments:	Pub at Walderton; pub at Westbourne; pubs, shops and cafes at Emsworth.
Conditions:	Delightful walking (albeit much of it on roads) through unspoilt scenery at the foot of the Sussex Downs, climaxing in the pretty town of Emsworth and the splendid Chichester Harbour. Note that in prolonged dry weather the river won't be flowing. The walk is best undertaken in the early months of the year.

Following the river: From the bus stop at the junction of the B2147 with the Stoughton road at Walderton, follow the Stoughton road through the centre of Walderton and out into open country beyond. Half a mile or so from the centre of Walderton you pass Mitchmere Farm which lies to your left, and a little beyond that, also to your left, is a roadside pond which is the source of the Ems. Now retrace your steps, heading back towards Walderton and beginning your journey proper towards the mouth of the river at Emsworth. The infant Ems may not appear hereabouts even after wet

Parallel courses - the river Ems as it hugs the Stoughton-Walderton road near to its source.

41

weather; looking into the field and then the gardens of Mitchmere Farm you can during "dry" periods see what is first a grassy channel then a more stony one marking the notional course of the river. Just beyond the farm and its grounds a track goes off to the right. Follow this track and then go through the first gate on the left, allowing you access to the left bank of the river; to begin with, it is possible that the Ems at this point may be only a trickle, but soon you reach a bigger pool of water and from that there should, following an average winter's rainfall, be a more substantial flow. Continue along the bank until the next field boundary forces you round to a gate that leads you back to the road, and from here you proceed along the road back to Walderton, the river running parallel with the road to your right. As you reach the village centre you temporarily lose sight of the river (it splits into two channels here, one on each side of the road), are then reunited with it by a tiny green, but lose it again behind the backs of houses to your right. Pass the popular Barley Mow pub and head away from the village centre; as you do so the river reappears to your right and makes a very picturesque sight indeed. At first the road is separated from the river by an area of rough grass and some subsidiary channels – it's possible to detour along sections of the bank before being forced back to the road – but soon the river runs right beside the road, having turned from a trickle into a determined stream. Continue to the junction with the Petersfield road.

Turn right at the junction and walk along the side of the road past the bus stop, then take the first left-hand turn along a narrow metalled road between houses. As the road bends very slightly to the right, turn left at a footpath sign and cross a field in the direction shown by the sign, aiming for a stile at the next field boundary. Cross the stile

Looking towards Racton on the river Ems on a crisp winter's afternoon.

The pretty town of Emsworth, offering ample refreshment opportunity for river Ems walkers.

and turn immediately left, following the field boundary round; as you swing to the right, you can clearly see the river to your left, and get an overview of the course taken by it from the Petersfield road. You now enjoy a delightful walk along a well-defined path, keeping the river immediately to your left. You approach the buildings of Lordington and arrive at a drive leading to the main buildings; the river goes underneath this drive, its passage facilitated by a charming mini-waterfall. Turn left onto the drive, then on arrival at the road turn right and follow it. Pass the left turn signposted Funtington and Chichester; just beyond the turning the river runs underneath the road so it is now to your left, and at this point there is an attractive pool into which the tributary stream flows. This really is a charming spot, especially on a sunny day following heavy rain. Now continue along the road, signposted Westbourne and Emsworth, with the river beside you to your left. You pass the very pretty little village of Racton, which boasts a splendid thatched timber-framed house with 17th century origins, and a church with features which date back to the 12th and 13th centuries. Inside the church are some impressive monuments including one dedicated to Sir George Gunter and dating back to the 17th century; it was one Colonel Gunter, believed to be Sir George's son, who helped the future King Charles II flee to France following the Battle of Worcester. Racton's most distinctive and conspicuous building is Racton Tower, a folly built in 1772 by Theodosius Keene. Soon you cross back over the river and climb away from the valley, enjoying views of the river as you rise. Follow the road to a T-junction at which you turn right, then descend along the road, bearing left into Foxbury Lane; you continue along the road, with good views to the now quite wide river through the vegetation to your right, and the houses of Westbourne village now in view.

When you reach the Cemetery Lane turning to the left, bear right, immediately opposite, along a signed footpath which takes you into the outskirts of Westbourne. Almost at once the path enters new development, so at the junction with the estate road bear right, then left, and then proceed along a straight road, Mill Road, flanked by older housing and with a recreation ground and allotments beyond this housing to the right. There is no access to the river from here so stay with the road. At the end you come to a T-junction at which you turn right, then walk along the road past a social club and school, soon arriving at the splendid house named Watersmeet, once a watermill. By looking to the right here, you'll see the river coming up to Watersmeet and you can observe how it passes under the road and then widens as it merges with a tributary stream. It's worth detouring on up the road beyond Watersmeet to the hamlet called Commonside, since from here you can enjoy a fine walk beside this tributary stream which originates from the a series of ponds just north-west of the hamlet of Aldsworth. By taking the (signed) Aldsworth road you'll shortly arrive at the most south-easterly of these ponds, as well as a charming waterfall. Retrace your steps to Watersmeet and keep walking along this road, keeping the Ems to your right. Almost immediately the river is lost to view and although you can detour at the next right turn to reach a charming bridge over the river, you won't be able to follow it again until you've passed the parish church at Westbourne.

Keep walking in the same direction to arrive in the centre of the pretty village of Westbourne, with a 14th century church, a number of old and picturesque houses and a wide variety of amenities. Proceed towards the church, indisputably the village's focal

The waterfront at Emsworth, where the river Ems flows into Chichester Harbour.

point, pass to the left of it and go on a little further, then bear left to a follow the path proceeding parallel with and to the left of a stream. Soon you arrive at a T-junction with a track onto which you turn right, following it as it proceeds pleasantly beside the stream then crosses over the A27. You keep to the track you're on, which bears round to the right to pass some large houses, then turn right along a path signposted Sussex Border Path(a little more detail on this is given in the chapter devoted to the East Sussex Rother), crossing the Ems once more; although the bank hereabouts is inaccessible, the surroundings are delightful. Soon you reach a T-junction of paths at which you turn left, passing under the railway bridge to enter the charming Brook Meadow. You come to a signboard giving details of wildlife in the meadow, and at this point you turn left and cross a footbridge over the Ems. You're now able to follow the bank, enjoying a very pleasant riverside stroll, but this ends rather disappointingly when you reach the A259 and lose the river again. Don't swing to the left with the path, but rather turn right through the underpass then left to walk parallel with the A259, heading eastwards. Turn right into Queens Road and join the first signed footpath on the left which takes you past some new housing and then onto an embankment, with Slipper Mill pond to your left and the Ems on your right; you can actually see the river reappearing from under the buildings on Queens Road. Keep along the embankment until it swings left. From this point you can see the Ems joining a wider channel which in turn leads into the clearly visible Chichester Harbour, and this prospect makes for a very satisfying end to your walk. Retrace your steps to Queens Road then turn left along this road to enter the town centre of Emsworth with its many amenities including three cafes. To get to the railway station, carry on up to the A259 roundabout, cross straight over and you'll see the station a few hundred yards up the road on your left.

THE RIVER KIRD

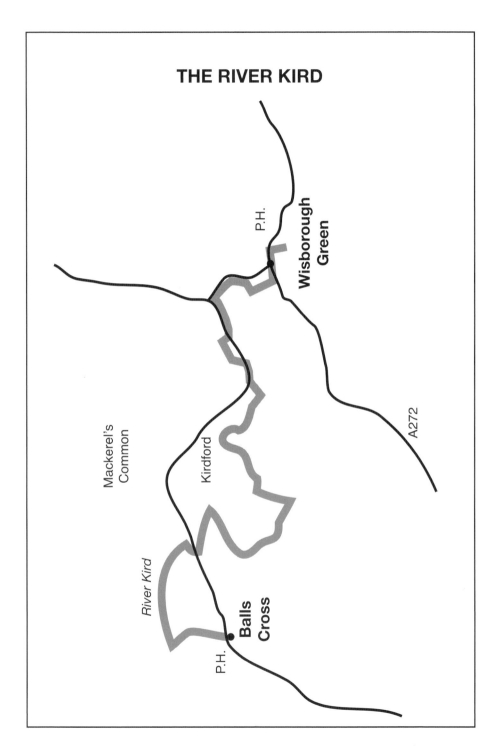

THE RIVER KIRD

Length:	9 miles.
Start:	Balls Cross.
Finish:	Wisborough Green.
Public transport:	Regular buses run between Balls Cross and Wisborough Green on a route that also serves Petworth, Billingshurst and Horsham (not Sundays); Billingshurst is on the Arun Valley railway line linking Chichester, Bognor Regis, Arundel and Pulborough with Horsham, Crawley and London.
Refreshments:	Pub at Balls Cross; pub and shop at Kirdford; Pub, shop and cafe at Wisborough Green.
Conditions:	Attractive walking in unspoilt countryside in the heart of Sussex between Petworth and Billingshurst. Unfortunately large stretches of the Kird are inaccessible for walkers, but there's plenty of most attractive path walking and there are several opportunities to view the river. A reasonably fit walker will accomplish this walk in a day and be able to pick up a bus in Wisborough Green back to the start or forward to Billingshurst.

Following the river: The Kird, one of the many tributaries of the Arun, is one of the less distinguished rivers of West Sussex, rising in remote countryside between the little villages of Ebernoe and Balls Cross a few miles north-east of Petworth. However Balls Cross is reasonably easy to reach by bus, other than on Sundays, and it is at the village pub, the Stag Inn, that your journey begins. Walk north-eastwards from the pub to the road junction in the middle of the village, and here turn left along the road signposted Ebernoe and Northchapel. You follow it for about three quarters of a mile, until on a downhill stretch in the shade of woodland you reach fingerposts pointing to public footpaths leading away on both sides. Take the signed path to the right, soon emerging from the trees, then pass through a gate and go straight across the field in the same direction, aiming for a gate on the other side. Pass through that gate and carry on along the path eastwards through more trees, emerging into a field with the buildings of Hilland Farm straight ahead. Swinging north-eastwards, follow the left-hand field edge,

A glorious spring afternoon on the banks of the river Kird.

and, taking care to observe the footpath signposts, carry on in the same easterly direction, passing well to the left of Hilland Farm and dropping down gently to arrive at the Kird for the first time, crossing it by a footbridge.

Beyond the footbridge you enter a field which may be muddy, and immediately turn right, swinging from north-eastwards to south-eastwards to follow alongside the Kird through the field, keeping as close to it as you can. In due course you're forced away from the Kird, using a footbridge to cross a small tributary stream and enter woodland, following the footpath signposts as you proceed south-eastwards. Emerge from the woodland then follow the left-hand field edge all the way to the Balls Cross-Kirdford road onto which you turn right. In a few hundred yards turn left onto a metalled track leading to Idolsfold Farm, but in fact you could detour to the very pretty Isling Bridge where the road crosses the Kird, before returning to the Idolsfold Farm track.

Follow the track up to a pond close to the farm buildings, proceed anti-clockwise round the pond to a stile, then observing the signposts, continue round the north side of further houses and walk along a clearly marked path through fields. Initially you head just south of east, then swing just north of east, along a right-hand field edge with woodland to your right. Beyond the woodland the marked path continues in the same direction through an open field, but you should turn right immediately beyond the woods and follow the right-hand field edge just west of south uphill, keeping the woodland to your right. There is no footpath as such but access is not a problem. Arriving at the top right-hand corner of the field you will see a footpath sign pointing south-westwards and you take this signed path along a right-hand field edge; you should be able to make out a lake and farm buildings immediately ahead of you, and you should aim for a point between the lake and the farm, here returning to the Kird valley. Descend gently to a footbridge over the Kird, from which you're able to follow with your eyes the course of the Kird upstream back towards Isling Bridge, and downstream towards Kirdford. Cross the bridge to enjoy a fine view of the Kird valley; while lacking the charisma of the Arun or Adur valleys, the mixed surroundings of unspoilt pasture and woodland make a most pleasing prospect. Beyond the footbridge, rise gently, passing just to the right of the lake and to the left of Crawfold Farm buildings, aiming for a multi-signed footpath fingerpost just beyond the top right corner of the field beyond the buildings. Having passed through one metalled kissing gate to enter this field, you pass through a second one to arrive at a T-junction with a wide grassy track onto which you turn hard left, following the track south-eastwards. The Kird valley is now once again lost to view but the walking, though unspectacular, is still most agreeable, with rolling fields to your left and woodland immediately to your right, and the track itself though undulating is very well-defined. Your track swings from south-eastwards to eastwards, another (private) track coming in from the right to join yours, but then swings south-eastwards again and enters a charming area of woodland. Ignoring a signed path going off to the right you keep to the track, going gently uphill and emerging from the woodland, then shortly turn left onto a signed path that proceeds along a right-hand field edge, fractionally east of north. Now the Kird valley comes once more into view; as it does so, watch carefully for and take a signed 90 degree right turn, the path now following a clearly defined track going just north of east, but very soon a signpost points your path off the track to the left. You pass through the middle of one field then, following the signing carefully, you continue along the right-hand edge of the next field. This is lovely walking, with views to Kirdford

Labour of love - one of many beautifully constructed river bridge crossings in Sussex. This one is a crossing of the Kird just outside Kirdford.

village ahead and the Kird valley to your left, and the river itself only a short distance below you. In fact you may find yourself able to detour to the bank, before being forced back to the path again, though by sticking to the path you get a better overview of the valley. You pass to the right of some hen coops then shortly are directed hard right along a narrow enclosed path which very shortly brings you to a road. Turn left onto it and descend gently to a bridge over the river, then continue into the centre of Kirdford. Kirdford is a rather sprawling community but has many attractive houses, particularly

in the vicinity of the popular pub and church of St John the Baptist, the nave and chancel of which date back to the 12th century. To continue, follow the path to the south of the church through the churchyard, enjoying superb views towards the Kird valley in the foreground, and ahead to the South Downs escarpment in the far distance. Beyond the churchyard the path does a 90-degree turn to the right, then snakes round the left-hand side of some buildings to arrive at a track; turn left onto the track towards an area of woodland, follow the signed path just east of south through the woods, then, emerging from the trees, continue in the same direction as signposted along a lovely path, a green carpet through fields, and past the left-hand edge of a lake. As you arrive at another area of trees you can see a road ahead, but rather than making straight

Time to seek the Lord? The west tower, complete with clock, in the historic church at Kirdford, just above the river Kird.

for it your path bears right and only then drops gently down to meet the tarmac. Although you can turn right on to the road to view the Kird as it passes under this road at Linfold Bridge, you then need to retrace your steps along the road and follow it north-eastwards to a T-junction with the Kirdford-Wisborough Green road.

Turn right onto the road and follow it for a little under half a mile, then turn hard left onto a signed footpath up a metalled track which heads initially westwards then swings northwards and eastwards. Soon after swinging eastwards the wide track comes to an end and you arrive at a junction of paths; take the right-hand path and now enjoy a delightful walk along a narrow way through woodland, passing a small lake and then walking roughly parallel with but above Boxal Brook, a tributary of the Kird. This is a really beautiful walk, and it's a shame when the path slips south-eastwards to arrive back at the Kirdford-Wisborough Green road. It's worth looking across at the pretty bridge carrying the brook underneath the road before turning left and following the road towards Wisborough Green, ignoring the Loxwood road turning to the left. Your road bends round to the right, passing under a row of pylons soon after which is a signed footpath to the right; follow this path as signposted, initially past buildings then through a field, along a left-hand field edge south-westwards towards a strip of woodland. At the edge of the woods, turn left as signposted to follow a path along the right-hand field edge on the east side of the wood. It is super walking, on a natural platform from which you can look down through the trees to the Kird valley and the river itself meandering through the meadows. You rise slightly to reach a T-junction with a track; turn hard right onto the track conveying you south-westwards to arrive at the A272, and by turning right here you will soon arrive at Green Bridge where the Kird passes under the A272. Disappointingly you cannot join the bank on either side, and you're forced to retrace your steps along the A272. This is a busy road, but you do at least have a pavement and it's only a few minutes' walk from here to the centre of Wisborough Green, a very pretty village indeed. As its name implies, it boasts an impressively wide green fronted by attractive vegetation and typical Wealden brick-built, half-timbered and tile-hung houses. Its large and imposing 11th century parish church has an unusual dedication, namely to St Peter ad Vincula, translated as "St Peter in chains," the chains being those in which St Peter was held when a prisoner of Herod Agrippa and which are thought to have had miraculous properties.

Follow the A272 past the church, looking out for a path leading up to the rectory which stands immediately adjacent to the church. Virtually opposite this path, and heading away from the A272 southwards, is a signed public bridleway. Turn right off the main road onto the bridleway which descends to arrive at a bridge crossing of the Kird. This is the last time you will be able to observe the Kird at such close quarters, and you may decide to end your walk here, simply backtracking to Wisborough Green for refreshment and a bus home. However if you wish to see a little more of the Kird valley and observe its confluence with the Arun, keep on along the bridleway, gently rising and getting good views to your left across the valley through which the Kird flows. You pass some buildings and lose sight of this valley, but shortly you begin your descent to the Arun valley; the metalled track gives way to a dirt track, well-defined but muddy in places, and you now drop decisively to arrive at a bridge over the Arun. Continue beyond the bridge to a crossroads of paths, where you meet the Wey South Path. Turn left here onto the Wey South Path, and now follow it back to the A272 at Newbridge using the reverse of the route as described in the chapter devoted to the Arun. The meeting of the Kird and Arun is across the river to the left a short way upstream. When you arrive back at the A272 at Newbridge, turn left for Wisborough Green or right for Billingshurst, there being little to choose distance-wise between these options.

Part of the magnificent tapestry on display inside the church at Wisborough Green near the point where the Kird meets the Arun.

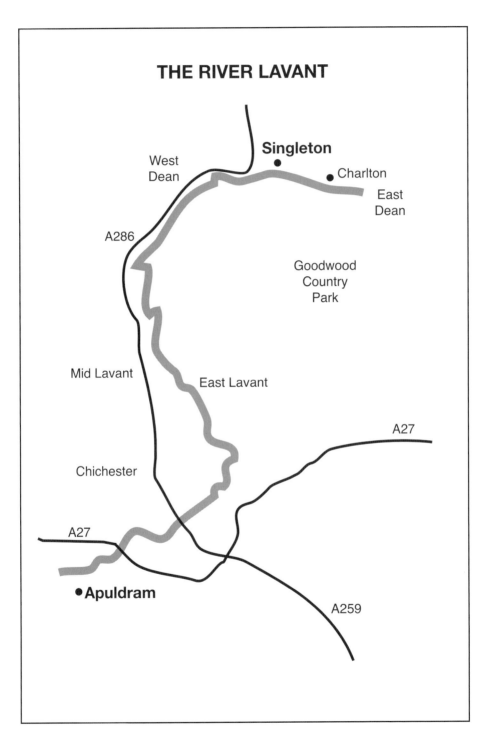

THE RIVER LAVANT

Singleton

West Dean

Charlton

East Dean

A286

Goodwood Country Park

Mid Lavant

East Lavant

A27

Chichester

A27

•Apuldram

A259

THE RIVER LAVANT

Length:	9 miles.
Start:	Singleton village centre.
Finish:	Chichester Harbour just west of Appledram.
Public transport:	Regular buses to Singleton from Chichester and Midhurst; trains from Chichester to Portsmouth, Brighton and London.
Refreshments:	Pub at East Dean; pub at Charlton; pub and café/shop at Singleton; pub and shop at West Dean; pub and shop at Lavant; pubs, shops and cafes at Chichester.
Conditions:	Easy, if occasionally muddy, walking between beautiful flint-built villages in the shadow of the Downs, culminating in the fine city of Chichester and its picturesque harbour. Note, however, that this is a winterbourne river, which is usually dry in the summer and only normally flows in the early months of the year, and it cannot be guaranteed even then that the river will be flowing throughout its length.

Following the river: If you're reliant on public transport, you'll need to begin from Singleton, as there is no regular bus service to the source of the Lavant at East Dean. Take the road signposted to Charlton and East Dean leading eastwards off the A286 Midhurst-Chichester road, and follow it for 2 miles to the centre of East Dean. East Dean is a very pretty place, with a beautiful setting beneath the South Downs, many attractive cottages of flint, a green and All Saints Church which dates from the 12th century. There is a pond in the village centre from which you can clearly see the channel of water, crossed by a picturesque bridge, heading away from it back towards Singleton. The river quickly bends northwards, away from the roadside and round the backs of houses; you retrace your steps back towards Singleton along the road, and once you've left the village, you'll soon see the river reappearing on your right. In a mile you reach Charlton, and as you come into the village, the river goes under the road and after following briefly parallel with it to the left, briefly disappears out of sight. Keeping to the road, you pass the popular Fox Goes Free pub and continue along it to Singleton, the river returning to the roadside and remaining beside it until, as you arrive in the village,

The infant river Lavant between Charlton and Singleton.

the river goes underneath the road. Just beyond this point, the road swings to the right; follow the road until you reach the village centre, with the village pond to your left and the river, hitherto separated from the road by houses, now clearly visible to your right and making a most picturesque sight. Singleton is a gem of a place, with many lovely flint-built cottages, a fine pub and a large church which boasts a Saxon tower and some interesting tombs and monuments. The village is perhaps best known for its superb Weald & Downland Open Air Museum, one of the most interesting museums in the country with its rich array of lovingly reconstructed buildings and many exhibitions depicting rural life down the centuries.

Go forward to the A286 and turn left to follow beside it towards Chichester, the river running initially parallel with the road and to its right. Fortunately there is a pavement available. Initially the river is to your right, just a short distance from the road and visible through the hedgerow, then crosses underneath the road and runs to the left of it. Soon after the river changes sides you turn left along a metalled drive signposted West Dean Gardens. Follow it straight on parallel with the river, going over a crossroads of tracks, but just beyond a small many-faced flint building with a thatched top, turn left along a track that passes a parking area, crosses the river and goes through a gate. Beyond the gate turn right and now proceed through a delightful area of parkland, initially walking immediately to the left of a wooded area. However soon you find yourself with the river just to your right, and you now enjoy a quite delightful riverside walk, with parkland to your left which rises towards the hilltops of Goodwood. Keep going beside the Lavant, with West Dean Gardens and the imposing early 19th century flint-built

West Dean College to your right on the other side of the river. Just level with the southern end of the college buildings you arrive at a cattle grid and kissing gate; turn right to pass through this gate, and now follow the metalled track back towards the house. Just before you reach it, turn left to follow a path which passes to the side of the building and on through a door in the flint wall just to the left of the church which though largely rebuilt following a fire in 1934 retains some pre-Norman features. Beyond the door, turn left to join a little road that goes back down to the river, now at the foot of West Dean village. This road which keeps just to the right of the river is quite delightful, the scene enhanced by the riverside green area and a charming little flint bridge. The popular Selsey Arms pub, actually on the A286, is easily reachable from here by means of a road leading uphill from the riverside road. Note that West Dean college and gardens are not always accessible to visitors, and if access is not possible you will need to keep to the A286, and turn left into West Dean village just beyond the signed route to the college.

The road which you have followed from the church heads towards a bridge crossing over the river. Turn right onto the last metalled road leading off shortly before the bridge, and climb to the A286; as you reach it, you will see a metalled footpath/cycleway known as the Centurion Way signposted to the left, effectively running parallel with the A286, and you follow this path, enjoying the views to the Lavant valley floor. At the hamlet of Binderton turn left with the Centurion Way and descend gently to cross the river,

The bubbly river Lavant in the delightful grounds of West Dean College.

57

going forward along the Centurion Way to join and follow the course of the old Chichester-Midhurst railway. This is a fine walk, the river Lavant to your right albeit some distance away. However, before long you see the river coming in from the right and less than half a mile from the point at which you joined the old railway line you reach a bridge crossing of the river. Immediately before the bridge turn left and follow the river bank through a field; this isn't shown on maps as a public footpath but is easily accessible nonetheless. The ground begins to rise and you cease to be able to follow the river bank, so, keeping in roughly the same direction, climb gently through the field to arrive at a hillside path, and turn right to follow it. Very soon you find yourself looking down on the River Lavant from above, and you'll also pass above a quite delightful pool from which a small tributary stream flows into the Lavant; set in the shade of trees, it is a most idyllic spot. The track now descends to the valley floor and you're able to return to the bank and continue southwards along the bank towards the village of Lavant. Shortly the wide track which brought you off the hillside goes away from the river, but you can continue along the bank of the river, following a narrow path; this isn't marked on maps as a right of way but at the time of writing was easily accessible. To your left are open fields, and to your right, immediately across the river, are the houses of Mid Lavant village. Look out for the imposing building which used to be Lavant railway station on the Chichester to Midhurst line; in common with other stations on the old railway line, it incorporated impressive mock timber-framing and moulded stucco panelling into its construction, and is now a private dwelling. Beyond that building, your narrow path swings to the left, a little away from the river, and proceeds via a field edge to arrive once again at the track that brought you down from the hillside. Turn right onto the track,

The river Lavant near Binderton, with a fine backcloth of the Kingley Vale nature reserve.

The positively snake-like meanders of the river Lavant between Binderton and the village of Lavant.

shortly reaching and turning left onto the metalled Sheepwash Lane, now in the village of East Lavant, and continue to a T-junction with Pook Lane. The river here, to your left, makes a particularly attractive sight.

Turn left onto Pook Lane, immediately crossing the bridge over the river, then take the first road turning on the right, Fordwater Road; this is almost exactly opposite the path leading to St Mary's Church, which boasts a 12th century nave and a 17th century brick tower. Follow Fordwater Road for a few hundred yards, very soon reaching a right-hand turn, Fordwater Lane, which you go past, then walk round a sharp left-hand bend immediately beyond. Just past the bend the right-hand verge widens a little, and almost at once you reach a house; just beyond the house there is a signed public bridleway, Stocks Lane, leading off to the right, which you follow. This is a most pleasant path, with good views across the Lavant valley, visible immediately on your right, to the suburban housing development of Summersdale and the huge Victorian tower of Graylingwell Hospital. Meanwhile, to your left is Goodwood motor racing circuit and airfield, and on fine days you should expect to see low-flying aircraft taking off or coming in to land. The path is wide and well defined, but can get very waterlogged after rain. In due course it bends in a more easterly direction, away from the Lavant valley, but you continue to follow it, emerging at a T-junction with Madgwick Lane. Turn right to follow it downhill; although it is classified as a minor road it is very busy, so take care. In due course you pass the old Westhampnett Mill which is to your right, and you will also become aware of a ditch immediately to your right, which is in fact an arm of the river Lavant although even if the main river is flowing this may remain dry. Proceeding parallel with this ditch you come to a roundabout junction, with a leisure complex immediately on your right; take the right-hand exit and go forward to a further roundabout, bearing right here into Barnfield Drive, passing The Barn restaurant and Homebase store, soon arriving at a bridge over the main course of the Lavant. Just before the bridge, turn left to join a concrete pedestrian/cycle track proceeding parallel with the river heading downstream, keeping the river to the right and the Homebase car park to your left; note the unusual sculptures that have been placed close to this track. The track bends right to cross a bridge over the river, then continues away from the river towards a housing estate. Just before the track enters the housing estate, look out for a narrow stony path leading away from the metalled track to the left; follow this path and continue along it as it swings to the left, then take the first right turn off the path to cross the river and arrive at Westhampnett Road. Cross the road and turn right to follow alongside it. In due course the road turns itself into St Pancras; the river is beside you for a time, first to your right and then to your left, but is soon lost to sight behind houses. Soon you reach the start of a one-way system where you bear left, shortly reaching a bridge over the Lavant which is visible to your left. This is the last you will see of the Lavant for a little while, for as the river proceeds from here towards the centre of Chichester it disappears beneath buildings.

At the bridge, cross the road and now bear round to the right, going forward into the Hornet, and proceeding on to a crossroads at Eastgate Square controlled by traffic lights.

The houses of the village of Lavant, looking out onto the river of the same name.

From here the buildings and shops of central Chichester are clearly visible ahead of you, but this is not your route; instead turn left into Market Avenue, keeping to the right-hand side as you proceed south-westwards along this road. As you near the end of this road and approach a T-junction with another one-way system, you'll see the river briefly reappearing to your right, and in spring the bank is bedecked with snowdrops, crocuses or daffodils. Just here, look straight ahead towards the modern redbrick Christ Church, and rather than going on to the T-junction at the end of Market Avenue you go forward to Christ Church passing immediately to the right of the front entrance. Continue along the road to a T-junction with South Street, the closest you will get to the very centre of the city of Chichester. Whole books have been written about the historic treasures of Chichester, the highlight of which is the city's magnificent 11th century cathedral with its Norman sculptures, shrine of St Richard, imposing 15th century Arundel Screen, and Marc Chagall's stained glass window. There are many other beautiful buildings in the city, including the fine 17th century Edes House in West Street, the 18th century Council House in North Street, the 500-year-old Cross, and the early 19th century Buttermarket, also in North Street. The city also has a wide variety of excellent shops and eating places.

Cross over South Street and turn left, then very shortly bear right down a lane opposite a cycle shop, and soon you'll see the river reappearing to your right; go forward in the same direction, just north of west, along the signposted Walls Walk, the river beside you and to your right throughout. Soon you reach a main road, the Avenue de Chartres, which you cross straight over, then keep going in the same direction, now on the grassy grounds of Chichester College, the river to your right. The river is temporarily lost to sight; to return to it, continue on the grass as far as you can then join a concrete drive which takes you to the main thoroughfare past the college buildings, walking along it till you reach D Block. You can now clearly see the river to your right. Cross the river by the bridge and enter the main college car park through which you proceed to the main exit, then turn hard left into Via Ravenna and follow this road back towards Chichester, soon crossing back over the river. Just beyond the river crossing, go briefly forward to cross the railway by the footbridge, then continue along the marked path between the units of the Terminus Road industrial estate. You cross Terminus Road and proceed to the A27 Chichester bypass which you cross as directed by the signs, taking immense care. Once over the road, you'll see the the river reappearing to your right and you can now follow parallel with the river almost all the way to its mouth. Shortly you reach a footbridge over the river and having crossed it, you could follow the signed path which runs parallel to and to the right of the river as it continues just south of west. However you can proceed immediately adjacent to, and to the right of, the river, and although this is not a designated right of way there should be no difficulty of access. Whichever route you choose, you come to a bridge which you cross, then continue along the path keeping the river now to your right. Cross a metalled road and proceed along the signed path in roughly the same direction, keeping the river to your right; it snakes away from the path a little, and you may be tempted to try and follow it, but if you do so, you should beware of a number of subsidiary channels which may impede your progress, and in the end you're forced back to the path. At length you reach the bank running beside Chichester Harbour and can enjoy lovely views to the harbour itself and back to Chichester Cathedral. By turning right you will soon arrive at the mouth of this fascinating, capricious river Lavant.

There's no obvious short cut back to Chichester city centre, but instead of retracing your steps, you could on reaching the harbour turn right to follow the harbourside in an inland direction up to Fishbourne; this is a really lovely walk, with beautiful views across the harbour and beyond to the Kingley Vale Nature Reserve and the Trundle. On reaching the end of Mill Lane leave the harbourside path and turn right up Mill Lane to reach the T-junction with the A259. Turn right to follow the A259 eastwards through the village, looking out for a footpath/cyclepath sign pointing away from the road under the main A27. Take this path that proceeds through the tunnel, then continue along the road, Fishbourne Road East; where this road bends to the right, go straight on over the railway and continue in the same direction, going forward to the mini-roundabout. Go straight across the mini-roundabout into Westgate, following this road to the roundabout junction with the Chichester ring road, crossing over into West Street and proceeding past the cathedral to the city Cross. Turn right into South Street to access the railway and bus stations.

The river Lavant near Chichester, with the cathedral spire of the city in the background.

*A typically winding stretch of the river Lavant in unspoilt countryside
between Lavant and Chichester.*

THE RIVER MOLE

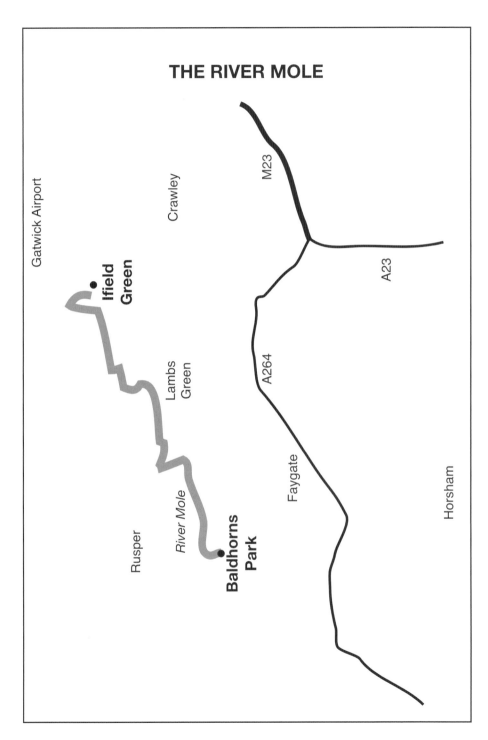

THE RIVER MOLE

Length:	(from start of bridlepath to Stafford Bridge): 5 miles.
Start:	Bridle path at west end of Baldhorns Park.
Finish:	Stafford Bridge, Ifield.
Public transport:	Regular buses between Horsham and Crawley via Faygate; regular buses from just above Stafford Bridge to Crawley (not Sund); regular trains from Ifield to Crawley and Horsham.
Refreshments:	Pub at Lambs Green; pubs and shops at Ifield.
Conditions:	A straightforward walk through countryside that is pleasant rather than beautiful. Towards the end the noise of planes taking off from or landing at nearby Gatwick can be intrusive.

Following the river: The River Mole is more associated with Surrey, and for many the enduring image of the Mole is the river crossing by stepping stones just below Box Hill near Dorking; indeed, it is only when it arrives in Surrey that it widens into a river of significance, and its course through Surrey is outside the scope of this book. It does however rise in Sussex, so I have included its course through the county for the sake of completeness, although it isn't a massively rewarding walk. During its journey through Sussex it does widen from its initial trickle but not significantly so, and it's impossible to follow for the latter stages of its course through the county; you can follow it a little beyond Stafford Bridge – the suggested finish of the walk – but surrounding vegetation and then the entering of the river into the Gatwick Airport complex means you cannot follow it on to the border with Surrey at Horley on the north side of the airport. However, there are compensations. The walk passes through attractive countryside, there is a church just off route with some interesting historical features, and plane-spotting walkers may in fact enjoy watching and identifying the aircraft almost directly above them.

The best place to start your walk is Faygate station; although trains serve the station very infrequently, there are regular daily buses there from Horsham and Crawley. Walk northwards from the station up Faygate Lane then at the next crossroads turn left into Wimlands Lane and, at the next junction, right into Wimland Road, following this road to a sharp left bend. Here you join a signed bridlepath and follow it just north of east, soon passing a pond to your left which is effectively the source of the Mole. Beyond

Even when you're forced away from the riverbank there's still lots to see; your writer was somewhat surprised to discover these two alpacas on his river Mole walk.

here you keep the infant Mole to your left, passing through the pleasant surroundings of Baldhorns Park. You arrive at a concrete bridge over the Mole with a gate straight ahead; don't go through the gate but turn sharp left, cross the bridge, then turn immediately right onto a signed path, keeping the Mole now to your right. In a few hundred yards you see a tempting track straight ahead, but you ignore this, rather bearing slightly right along a signed path back over the Mole and continuing eastwards well to the south of Rusper Court Farm. Soon the bridleway becomes a metalled lane and, still proceeding eastwards, you go forward to a T-junction with Faygate Lane.

Turn left onto the lane, soon crossing the river again, then continue uphill along the lane. Just past Applegarth to the right, turn right onto a signed footpath which heads briefly north-eastwards then swings south-eastwards downhill through a field with good views to the Mole valley. Aim for the footbridge at the south-east corner of the field and cross it, then, following the direction shown by the fingerpost, go forward to arrive at a T-junction with a road at the hamlet of Lambs Green. Turn left to follow the road, passing the tempting Lamb Inn; the road bends sharply left and you then turn right onto a signed path a couple of hundred yards short of Lambs Green Bridge over the Mole (there's no access to the bank but it's worth detouring to the bridge to enjoy another glimpse of the river). Head eastwards along the path, which although not always clear on the ground is easy to follow with the help of the fingerposts and gates. In just under half a mile you are signposted half-left across a field aiming directly for the buildings of Stumbleholm Farm, then having crossed the field you go through the gate onto a concrete lane, with the very attractive farmhouse ahead. Turn left then almost immediately right along a signed path which passes the right edge of a strip of woodland to reach a T-junction of footpaths, bearing left here to go forward to reach a road.

Turn left onto the road, crossing over the Mole using Grantham Bridge. The river to your left looks particularly attractive here, in the shade of woodlands; note here a very conspicuous river feature, namely the river height indicator which in summer or during dry spells may seem somewhat redundant! Keep along the road to a sharp bend just ahead, turn right at this bend onto a minor road, then soon turn right on to a signed path. This heads fractionally south of east to the corner of an area of woodland where you meet the Mole again; now keeping the wood to your right and Bonwicks Place to your left, enjoy a pleasant walk alongside the Mole, before a fingerpost directs you left. Very soon you reach a footpath junction and a hedge, here bearing right to follow the signed path a fraction north of east, keeping the hedge hard to your left. Again the river comes in from your right, but don't be tempted into the woodland immediately adjoining it (the path is indistinct here); keep on to a footbridge which you cross, turning left to walk parallel with the Mole, enjoying good views across the meadow to Ifield Church. You pass a lovely area of woodland to your left, then immediately beyond the woods, turn left along a track, keeping the Mole still to your left. You soon arrive at a point where the main track veers to the left, over the Mole; turn right here and follow a clear path

Two deer enjoying a morning's exercise in the Mole valley near Lambs Green.

through a field to a footbridge* over another stream, immediately beyond which you reach a T-junction of paths. The main route is left, eastwards, but it's possible to turn right and then immediately left onto an obvious path heading for the lovely church of St Margaret, Ifield, which dates back to the 13th and 14th centuries. Its most notable features are the two 14th century effigies depicting Sir John de Ifelde and Lady Margaret de Ifelde. Returning to the main route continue eastwards from the footbridge marked * above, soon arriving at a road; turn left onto it, then when the road shortly bends right, go straight on along a lane heading northwards to a footbridge over the Mole. Cross over, and turn right to follow the Mole until you reach the hedge separating you from Charlwood Road. You then need to follow the field north-westwards beside the road until you reach a way out onto the road close by a turning for Ifield Hall; having finally accessed Charlwood Road, you turn right onto it and follow it south-eastwards, ignoring turnings to the right and left. Shortly after these turnings you reach the Stafford Bridge crossing of the Mole.

It's possible to cross the bridge and immediately turn left onto the right bank of the Mole, and enjoy a pleasant walk beside the river for about half a mile until the path, not marked on any OS maps, veers away from the river. The river continues on towards Gatwick but there's no possibility of any riverside walking from here on, so your walk returns to Stafford Bridge the same way. You may pick up a bus here, but to access Ifield Station you need to turn right onto the road, then take the first left turn into Ifield Green; at the T-junction you turn right into Warren Drive, then bear right at the next T-junction into Ifield Drive, heading slightly uphill to reach the station.

*A river height indicator placed in the river Mole, and looking somewhat
redundant on a dry spring morning!*

THE RIVER ROTHER (WEST SUSSEX)

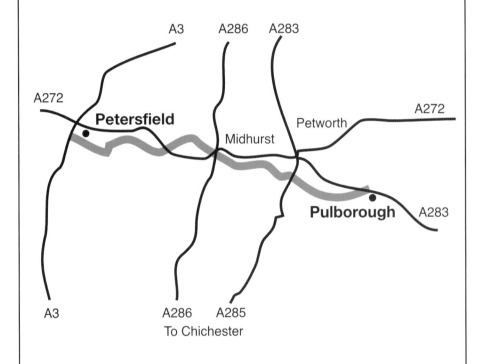

THE RIVER ROTHER (WEST SUSSEX)

Length:	Approximately 25 miles.
Start:	Petersfield.
Finish:	Pulborough.
Public transport:	Frequent trains serving Petersfield on the London Waterloo-Guildford-Haslemere-Havant-Portsmouth line; regular buses linking Petersfield with Midhurst via Rogate; regular buses from Pulborough to Petworth, Midhurst and Worthing; rail services linking Pulborough with Arundel, Chichester, Horsham, Crawley and London.
Refreshments:	Pubs, shops and cafes at Petersfield; pub at Rogate; pub at Trotton; pub at Iping; pub at Stedham; pubs, shops and cafes at Midhurst; pub at Selham; pub at Tillington; pubs, shops and cafes at Petworth (off route); pub at Heath End; pub at Fittleworth; pubs, shops and cafes at Pulborough.
Conditions:	This is one of the more logistically challenging of the riverside walks described in this book. Although there is some fine scenery, only limited sections of the river bank are available to walkers, and those reliant on public transport will find the walk somewhat frustrating in places.

Following the river: This is not the only River Rother in Sussex, there being another Rother in East Sussex. The West Sussex River Rother is the widest and longest river in West Sussex that doesn't flow into the sea, but rather is a tributary of the Arun. It actually rises in Hampshire, some miles west of the Sussex border, and its flow through Hampshire is beyond the scope of this book. Your walk starts at Petersfield, which is very accessible by public transport, and only a shortish walk from the start of the Rother's journey through West Sussex. It's also a delightful town in its own right and worth stopping in before you set out, with a multitude of fine old buildings, interesting shops and excellent eating places.

Exit Petersfield railway station via the ticket office and go straight ahead down Lavant Street to the T-junction at the bottom with Chapel Street, turn right into Chapel Street and follow the road round to arrive at the attractive market square. Continue along the road, now High Street, and at the end pass straight over Dragon Street into Heath Road. Follow Heath Road just south of east, continuing along it as it bends sharply right and

A quiet corner in Midhurst, arguably the most historic and interesting town on the Rother in West Sussex.

arrives at a T-junction, with Heath Pond immediately ahead. Cross over towards the pond, but immediately bear left onto a clear path through the grassy pondside area, heading north-eastwards and running parallel with the road. In due course the path enters an area of woodland and emerges at Heath Road East, and here you cross straight over into Durford Road, and continue eastwards along this residential road. You reach a crossroads, with Penns Place leading off to the left; go straight over, still on tarmac but now along what is a cul-de-sac. After a couple of hundred yards beyond the Penns Place crossroads, the road becomes effectively a driveway and swings to the right; you bear left here and go forward to enter a field. Don't stick to the extreme right-hand field edge, but take a more diagonal route through it, aiming for a footpath fingerpost just to the left of a line of bushes. Here you

pick up an obvious path which takes you downhill to meet the Rother at a charming footbridge. Cross it, then make your way away from the river through the meadow, aiming for a stile straight ahead on the hillside. Go over the stile and bear right, continuing parallel with and slightly above the river. In a few hundred yards you reach another stile and footpath sign (note the picturesque Serpent Trail footpath waymark on the stile); turn right here over the stile and make your way across the meadow, aiming for the footbridge which you cross, then bear left.

The going is now straightforward and very pleasant, with the river close by you to your left. Initially you follow alongside it through open country, enjoying views to the Downs to your right, but shortly beyond a stile (at which you continue straight ahead) you become separated from the river by trees, although you stay parallel with the river and can see it through the trees. You continue through a field which in spring is a sea of yellow – the very common oilseed rape plant, not good news for hay fever sufferers! Keeping the river close by to your left, you make for the stile at the end of the field, and cross over it. The footpath now goes straight on through the next field, aiming for a gate*, but you could veer left just beyond the field and walk along all the way to the fence beyond which is a large house and extensive grounds, here going up to the gate marked * above. The riverside walk is extremely attractive but beware that it can be squelchy in places, even during dry spells. Cross the stile next to the gate marked *, and continue eastwards to a metalled driveway which in turn arrives at a T-junction with the West Harting-Middlemarsh road.

It is almost obligatory to detour to the left (northwards) along the road to the old bridge over the Rother; this is a delightful spot, the river looking wide and impressive after spells of heavy winter rain. Retrace your steps and proceed southwards back to the point you arrived at the road, then rise slightly and proceed past the old bridge crossing of the Midhurst to Petersfield railway. Immediately beyond it, bear left onto a signed footpath, which you follow parallel with the course of the railway. This is lovely walking, with good views to the Rother valley to the left, and to the Downs on your right. In half a mile you reach a T-junction of paths. Turn left to pass immediately to the left of a house, then, following the signpost, proceed along a left-hand field edge, shortly veering gently left through a small wooded area and going downhill. Cross a stile into the meadow, the river now immediately ahead of you. Bear round to the right, walk down to and cross the bridge and continue along the farm lane, slightly uphill, to reach the A272; turn right and follow alongside the A272 for just under a mile to arrive at Rogate. There is in fact a fairly wide grass verge so it shouldn't be necessary for you to walk on the tarmac.

On arrival at Rogate you take the first right-hand turn into Parsonage Estate, although you may wish to detour to the centre of the village with a useful shop, an interesting church parts of which date back to the 13th century, and a number of picturesque cottages. Back on the route, walk along the Parsonage Estate road and take the second turning off it on the right. Follow this subsidiary road to its very end, and go forward on to a path across a field; don't go across to the opposite end but bear right as directed by the footpath signpost, and follow the path gently uphill along the hillside, gradually swinging left and leaving the housing behind. At the crest of the hill you reach a junction of paths, here going straight over and proceeding southwards, downhill through the field aiming for the right-hand edge of an area of woodland. Cross a ditch by a plank bridge and proceed along the right-hand fringe of the wood, then, maintaining the same direction, continue downhill. You then pass to the right of an area of thicker vegetation, aiming for another footpath signpost in a marshy area on the valley bottom. At this signpost, turn sharp left, walking through the marshes and aiming for a footbridge over the river. Cross this footbridge and almost immediately arrive at a T-junction with a farm lane, turning left onto the lane and following it to a minor road at the hamlet of Habin. Although you turn right to continue, you may wish to detour left to reach Habin Bridge river crossing, originally built and maintained in the Middle Ages by a local religious community known as the Canons of Durford. Sadly this will be your last sight of the Rother for some while.

Follow the road briefly southwards from the bridge, shortly turning left onto a signed bridlepath, rising slightly and ignoring two paths soon going off to the right. Although you're some distance from the Rother hereabouts, the countryside is very attractive indeed, with fine views to the South Downs escarpment. Beyond the second path turning you descend then swing to the right and pass underneath a massive line of pylons; your path swings left, round the edge of a patch of woodland, then swings right again and goes steadily downhill to the Nyewood-Dumpford road. Turn left onto this road and follow it to Dumpford, then as you arrive in this small village, you pass a right turn leading to Elsted. Shortly after this turning, you bear left into Mill Lane and follow the road past houses, then as the road swings left, turn right onto a path that brings you to the pond at Dumpford Mill. Here you are reunited with the Rother, but don't get too excited as unfortunately there is no chance of access to the bank. Follow, therefore, the marked path up through a field, then ignoring a path forking left, proceed along the path that follows the left-hand edge of a field and widens into a track that goes forward to the A272 at Trotton. Turn right to follow the road to the bridge, controlled by traffic lights and because there is no pavement you need to be very careful as you continue over it. Like Habin Bridge, the medieval sandstone bridge at Trotton is a very fine construction indeed with its five semi-circular arches and four huge cutwater buttresses on either side; it was built by the 1st Lord Camoys who also built the village church. The church itself contains some important brasses and a memorial to the 17th century Restoration dramatist Thomas Otway.

Beyond the bridge, cross over to the north side of the A272 and very soon you will see a stile to your left indicating a signed path which you follow north-eastwards, rising and then following first the left-hand then the right-hand side of a barbed wire fence through a field on a hillside. The Rother is immediately below you to the left, and it is possible to follow the bank, but to get to it you need to walk through

West Sussex Rother-side walkers seeking literary inspiration, look no further - the delightful Wheeler's Bookshop in the heart of Midhurst.

an area of pasture which could be extremely squelchy following wet weather, and in any case you're then forced back to the marked path. This path proceeds north-eastwards to arrive at a minor road linking the A272 with Chithurst; turn left onto this road and follow it, soon coming to a signed path leading off to the right. Now* you have a choice. You could turn right onto this path and follow it eastwards to Iping; the path rises to allow superb views towards the South Downs to the right, and to the Rother through the woods. You then descend along the path and go past the backs of houses to arrive at Iping. Arriving at the road, turn left onto it, crossing the river by means of a sturdy five-arch bridge to arrive in the attractive village centre. Alternatively at * you could continue along the road to its bridge crossing over the Rother, taking the opportunity to visit the charmingly situated little church at Chithurst just beyond the bridge on the left, containing the original 11th century walls. A little beyond the church, turn right onto a signed path that proceeds to Iping on the north side of the Rother but remaining in the valley and emerging in the centre of the village. Notwithstanding the beauty of the church at Chithurst, the first route is better. If you decide on the latter route, it's worth detouring down to the bridge over the Rother at Iping so you can inspect the river as it runs through the village.

Whichever way you've arrived in Iping, you leave it by taking the track that proceeds eastwards away from the village street opposite the village notice board; it's easy and enjoyable walking, and the Rother is now clearly visible to the right. Continue along the track roughly parallel with the river, and in a few hundred yards you come to a footbridge over the river. There is no official public right of way across the bridge but there is apparently no difficulty of access, so cross the river then immediately turn left to follow a field edge parallel with the river, arriving at a T-junction with a bridleway. Turn left onto the bridleway and follow it. This is lovely walking in woodland; initially the path rises to give you a grandstand view of the Rother to your left, then descends to the road just above the village of Stedham. Your way is left, but it's worth detouring to the right to visit the village with its long street of brick and sandstone buildings, a church with a Gothic-style 17th century tower, and the impressive 17th century Stedham Hall north of the church. There's also a pub but it's at the far end of the village. Proceed briefly north-westwards along Stedham Lane, almost immediately crossing the 17th century six-arched bridge over the Rother, then just beyond the farm buildings of Bridgefoot turn right onto a signed public footpath. You're now able to walk immediately beside the Rother all the way to Woolbeding Bridge. In fine weather, this is an absolutely idyllic walk, providing some of the loveliest riverside walking in Sussex. You pass the beautiful waterfall by Stedham Mill then keep Woolbeding Wood to your left, ignoring signed paths leading into the woods; on one occasion you need to ascend then descend steps into and out of the wood, but otherwise you have the river for company throughout. Leaving the woodland behind, you enter a lovely area of meadow, and here in the spring there is a profusion of beautiful wild flowers, with hosts of bluebells, buttercups and cow parsley. Almost too quickly you arrive at the medieval triple-arched

Woolbeding Bridge; there is no way forward from the riverside to the bridge, and to get onto the bridge you need to turn left and follow the field edge parallel with the road to a stile which allows access to the road that in turn brings you back to the bridge.

From Woolbeding Bridge take the signed footpath which runs parallel with the right (south) bank of the river east of the bridge, then strikes out to the south-east and climbs to the A272 at its junction with June Lane. Turn immediately left into June Lane, now entering the town of Midhurst, and follow it all the way to the T-junction with North Street, Midhurst's main street. Midhurst is an extremely attractive town, offering the best range of amenities on this walk and boasting several very fine buildings including the magnificent part-16th century Spread Eagle Hotel and the 16th century Old Market House, but both South Street and Market Square in particular have many delightful old houses and shops. Turn left onto North Street and follow it northwards, going forward to the bridge over the Rother and its beautiful weir (note that there is no access to the bank on either side) and thence to the roundabout forming the junction of the A272 Petworth road and A286 Guildford road. Turn right off this mini-roundabout to follow a metalled drive through the Cowdray estate, keeping the Rother to your right, as far as the ruins of Cowdray House; the original house was developed in the 16th century but much of it was destroyed by fire in 1793. As you reach the Cowdray ruins, you'll see a river bridge to the right which you cross, then immediately turn left to follow a very attractive riverside path which draws many strollers and picnic parties. It is not surprising to learn that even today the Rother hereabouts is used for raft races and toy duck races! The path bends to the right, then at the next junction of paths a few yards beyond you take the path to the left, continuing to follow the riverside in the shade of trees. Over the river you have views to the polo fields of Cowdray Park that are a hive of activity in the summer months. You shortly arrive at an open area, with a road going off to the right; go forward to cross a bridge over a tributary stream, then immediately beyond the bridge, turn left onto a path that rises quite sharply. This is delightful walking, with attractive woodland to your left and glimpses to the river below, as well as lovely views to the Cowdray estate and the Downs. Keep to the path which loses sight of the river and becomes metalled, in due course arriving at a junction with the West Lavington-Ambersham road which you join, continuing in the same direction. You almost immediately cross a charming tributary stream then climb gently and pass the twin farmsteads of Great Todham and then Little Todham. This roadside stroll is extremely pleasant, even though you have temporarily parted company with the river. A little way beyond Little Todham bear left onto a signed footpath initially running parallel with the road and then branching off to the left. You descend and proceed quite delightfully parallel with the Rother and just above it; in the springtime the bank separating you from the river is carpeted with bluebells. Soon you descend to the river level and proceed to the road at Ambersham Bridge.

Turn right onto the road and follow it for just under half a mile to South Ambersham, ignoring the road branching off to the right, then at the road junction at South

Ambersham turn left to follow the road eastwards for a mile and a half to Selham. There's attractive countryside on both sides including polo fields to your right, and as you enter Selham you will observe its very pretty Norman church which also lies to your right. Arriving at the T-junction at Selham, you may be tempted to detour right to visit the Three Moles pub which has a reputation for superb real ale, but your way is left, keeping to the road. Continue along the road northwards from Selham to Lods Bridge over the river; you cross it, then almost immediately turn right onto a signed path which briefly follows a tributary stream at first and then joins the Rother. Follow it for half a mile or so, initially through meadows, but shortly beyond a stile you enter a more marshy area and your path veers left, away from the river, frequently using boardwalks. You reach a sort of boardwalk T-junction and bear left, aiming for a group of stumps; beyond the stumps, bear round to the right and at the edge of the trees you'll see a post with yellow footpath arrow. Head for this and follow the arrow's direction, uphill along a sunken path in the shade of trees, then go forward across an area of concrete with farm machinery to reach a metalled farm lane by a gate. Turn left and

follow this lane for just under half a mile to arrive at the A272 Midhurst-Petworth road. Turn right to follow alongside this road, passing a road turning to the left and a marked parking bay a little beyond that, then about 300 yards beyond the bay, close to the village of Tillington, you turn right onto a signed, potentially very muddy, footpath which proceeds between tall hedges and past some farm buildings. The footpath kinks right then left, suddenly narrowing and descending steeply to reach the Rother. Turn left to follow a path that runs roughly parallel with the Rother, initially ascending then abruptly dropping to arrive at a footbridge. Don't cross the footbridge but continue to follow the north (left) bank. Although this is not a designated right of way, access presents no problem and you are able enjoy a delightful riverside walk through lovely unspoilt

The West Sussex Rother at Midhurst, as it passes the Cowdray polo fields.

meadows. After about half a mile you arrive at another footbridge which you cross, and you now continue on the right bank of the river. You can follow this almost all the way to the A285 at the Badgers pub, passing the attractive farm buildings of Rotherbridge as you proceed. Within sight of the A285 you're forced to veer right, away from the river, up to a clear track; turn left onto the track which you follow to the A285, just a few yards to the right of the popular Badgers pub.

Turn left to follow beside the A285 past the pub and shortly cross a bridge over an "arm" of the Rother. This is a quite beautiful scene, with a weir to the right and the waters hereabouts surrounded by trees and lush vegetation. Immediately beyond the bridge is the Coultershaw Beam Pump which is well worth a visit if it is open. The pump was installed in 1790 by the 3rd Earl of Egremont for the purpose of raising water from the Rother to supply the town of Petworth, two miles away, and at the time was one of the earliest pumped water systems in existence. Proceed on alongside the A285 slightly uphill until, a couple of hundred yards beyond the beam pump, and opposite houses on the left, you turn right onto a metalled track and follow it, enjoying good views to the Rother valley to your right. The track kinks slightly to the left as it passes Hoes Farm but then continues in virtually the same direction. You come to another grouping of buildings where the track comes to an end, and to continue beyond the track you cross over a stile into a meadow. Proceed downhill, in precisely the same direction as you were taking along the track, then bear south-eastwards to reach a stream on the edge of

A welcome sight for thirsty West Sussex Rother-side walkers - the hugely popular Three Moles at Selham, renowned for its excellent beer.

a small area of woodland. Continue beside the stream along a path which could be very muddy after rain, then cross over another stile, going forward to a T-junction with a track. Turn left onto the track, almost immediately reaching a road onto which you turn right, then proceed uphill. Enjoy a lovely view of the Rother valley from the top, then descend along the road to Shopham Bridge over the river.

Cross the bridge and immediately turn left onto the signed footpath on the south side of the river. There now follows a delightful riverside walk along the bank, and although it isn't shown as a right of way on the map, access is permitted almost all the way to the Bury-Fittleworth road. The walking is most rewarding, with large expanses of meadow around you, and fine views on your right to the wooded South Downs escarpment and the masts on Bignor Hill. Look out for an assembly of attractive and quite striking buildings on the hillside to your left; as you get level with them, you should find yourself at a gate through a barbed wire fence extending across the meadow to your right. Bear right immediately beyond the gate to follow parallel with the east side of the fence, pass through a gate and go forward to a gap (formerly bridged) between two portions of embankment on the old Pulborough-Midhurst railway. Be warned – this could be exceedingly muddy! Continue in the same direction through the field and proceed to the kissing gate, here turning left on to Coates Lane and following it for about a quarter of a mile to the junction with the Bury-Fittleworth road, turning left onto the road. Descend slightly to an impressive bridge over the Rother.

Just before the bridge turn right onto a signed footpath, and follow it along the water's edge. Sadly you're forced away from the riverbank after about half a mile, but continue along the extremely well-signed path which leads you across fields and into woodland. After wet weather the wooded section floods very badly and in extreme conditions may be passable only with great difficulty. Assuming you emerge unscathed, you go forward to arrive back at the course of the Pulborough-Midhurst railway, then turn left to follow the old line eastwards. Although your walk along the line isn't marked as a right of way on maps, it is in fact a permissive path and the only section of the old line where automatic access has been granted to walkers. It's a lovely walk which provides frequent and wide-ranging views of the Rother valley to the left, and although the Rother's course isn't obvious, you perhaps get a better picture of the valley floor than you would if you were immediately beside the river. There are also good views to the South Downs escarpment to the right when the trees relent. Eventually the path arrives at the point where the old railway line left the still extant Arundel-Pulborough line, and you're directed by a signpost to the left, towards an accumulation of farm buildings and workings. Shortly you arrive at a T-junction with a metalled drive at which you turn right, and you now follow this drive to a T-junction with a metalled road linking the A29 with the Hardham waterworks. Turn left to follow this road through the waterworks, arriving at a footbridge over the Rother. If you look to the right here you will see towards its nearby confluence with the Arun, which itself can be seen just a couple of hundred yards ahead of you. Your pilgrimage along the Rother is now at an

end. The quickest way to the amenities and railway station at Pulborough is to follow north-westwards from the waterworks across the field to cross the Arun footbridge and then continue forward to the A283. Turn right onto the road and follow it for just over half a mile to reach the town.

Trees both dressed and bare - an autumnal sight on the West Sussex Rother just east of Lods Bridge near Selham.

*The imposing Cowdray Ruins, close to the banks of the West Sussex Rother,
on a sunlit autumn afternoon.*

THE RIVER BREDE / THE RIVER LINE

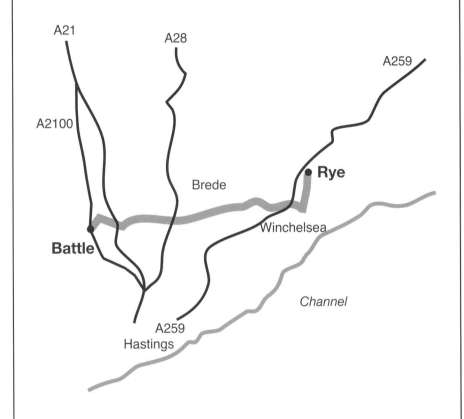

THE RIVER BREDE / THE RIVER LINE

Length:	16 miles.
Start:	Battle.
Finish:	Rye.
Public transport:	Regular trains on the London Charing Cross to Hastings line via Tunbridge Wells serving Battle; for Rye see under Tillingham.
Refreshments:	Pubs, cafes and shops at Rye; pub and shop at Sedlescombe; pub, shop and café at Winchelsea; pubs, shops and cafes at Rye.
Conditions:	This is two rivers for the price of one, so to speak: as well as walking beside the wide and impressive river Brede, you'll also be able to follow a small tributary river named the Line. For the most part, you can enjoy excellent riverside walking but there are two significant stretches where the river has to be forsaken. The countryside is magnificent and there is the bonus of three beautiful old towns, one at the start and one at the end of the walk, and a historic castle.

Following the river: Battle, where you walk begins, is one of the most interesting towns in Sussex and the site of the famous conflict in 1066 between King Harold and William The Conqueror. The town's most important historical feature is its Abbey, built by the victorious William in atonement for the blood he shed on the battlefield, and although the Abbey itself is now a ruin, its gatehouse contains examples of Norman, Gothic and early Renaissance architecture. The loveliest part of the town is Abbey Green, in front of the gatehouse, while facing out onto the green is the splendid half-timbered Pilgrim's Rest, dating from the 15th century. Other excellent buildings in the town include the Friar House which dates back to 1642, the 15th century timber-framed Almonry, the tile-hung Kings Head Inn and the part-16th century Langton House. The town is full of interesting shops and has two particularly fine museums, one within the Abbey complex and the other, Buckleys Yesterday's World, offering authentic displays of aspects of social history in a medieval hall-house, as well as an array of tempting merchandise which may deplete your reserves of cash not to mention add extra weight

The start of your walk alongside the pretty river Line, a tributary of the river Brede.

to your rucksack!

Walking up Battle's main street from the station, turn right along the Whatlington road, following it for about a mile and crossing over the railway. Shortly after this crossing the road drops to a bridge over the river Line, and here you can turn right to follow its right bank, soon using a footbridge to switch to the left bank, and, with a wide field to your left, proceed to arrive at the A21. Turn right to follow this busy road for about 100 yards then cross with great care and turn left onto a signed footpath which runs parallel with and to the right of a tributary stream. In due course the stream meets the Line and you then follow the right bank of that river, crossing it just before a children's play area then following the marked path on to the outskirts of Sedlescombe, keeping the play area to the right. Arriving at Sedlescombe's main street, you continue your riverside journey by turning right and proceeding to the bridge over the river. However, you should detour left to enjoy the village which slopes gently for nearly a mile up a hillside, its long triangular green lined with brick and tile-hung houses; just beyond the top of the green is Manor Cottages, a large timber-framed house with mullioned windows, which is believed to date in part from the 15th century, while the church, situated at the top end of the village, boasts a 15th century tower. One other feature of note at Sedlescombe is Oaklands, an estate to the south-east of the village, which was opened in 1959 as the Pestalozzi Children's Village for deprived children of all Third World countries. Having seen the village, go back to the river bridge, cross over it, and turn left to follow the bank; imperceptibly, the Line has become the Brede and it's this river you're now following. A signboard invites you to look out for barn owl, water vole, water crowfoot, lapwing, snipe, yellowhammer and chaffinch, as you keep along the bank using a very narrow path between the fence and the water.

Your fine riverside walk is rudely cut short after a little over half a mile where at a tributary channel you're forced to bear right. Walk alongside this channel, aiming for a stile and crossing it, then bear left and head for a stile at the edge of the woods. Cross this stile too and follow the clear path beyond it, then when the main path bears right, keep to the path nearest the north edge of the woods in the river valley. At this point the river and its valley can still be seen through the trees, but in due course the path swings right and, with no forward option, you're now forced away from the river. The path goes steeply uphill, emerging at a field edge; you enter the field but then turn left almost immediately and climb, aiming for a footpath sign ahead and going forward

beyond that sign to reach the road. Turn left and follow the road for just over half a mile. Pass under pylons and the entrance to Redlay Farm, the road now descending; as the road bends sharply to the right, bear left onto a signed path and follow the signs initially along a track then through fields, underneath another line of pylons, heading eastwards and aiming for a footbridge with footpath finger posts at the valley bottom. Cross the footbridge then turn left to follow a path bringing you back to the Brede. Don't cross the river footbridge here, but turn right immediately before it to follow the right bank along a permissive path to Brede Bridge. This is most pleasant walking, the river immediately beside you to the left and a charming pastoral landscape to the right,

Looking from the river Brede to the church in the village of the same name.

The peaceful course of the river Brede between Brede village and Winchelsea.

The railway crossing of the river Brede near Winchelsea, with the hill on which Winchelsea is built just discernible in the background.

although the path for all but the final few couple of hundred yards is not well defined and when I walked it after a warm wet spring it was not too easy to follow through lush growth including nettles and thistles. As you approach the bridge, look out for the fortress-like Brede Church on the hilltop to your left. Brede Bridge carries the busy A28 over the River Brede, so take care when crossing the road. You may wish to detour left up the A28 to visit the village of Brede, with a mixture of weatherboarding and brick at its centre. It's quite a climb from the valley, but in fact the church is well worth a visit: it dates back to 1140 and boasts a mid-15th century tower as well as a chapel which contains the tomb of Sir Goddard Oxenbridge who was rumoured to eat children for his supper. To continue towards Rye, walk on from Brede Bridge along the south (right) bank of the river, but in less than half a mile you're forced away from it by a wide tributary channel. Follow the channel south-westwards, crossing the footbridge then proceeding south-eastwards over the field to pass under the railway. Beyond the railway, there's a steep uphill climb through a field, heading south-eastwards, aiming for and passing to the right of the Lidham Hill farm buildings and emerging at a road. Turn left onto the road then, as it swings sharply right, bear left onto a track; this starts in a north-easterly direction then swings east. You now proceed just north of east along a reasonably clear path through fields, well signposted with distinctive red waymarks of the 1066 Country Walk, with which your journey coincides for this section. The 1066 Country Walk is a 31-mile walk linking Rye with Pevensey via Battle, retracing the steps of the invading Normans. Look ahead for the hilltop farm buildings of Lower Snailham, and as you get to the foot of the hill on which the farm is built, you cross a stream and bear right, south-eastwards, as directed by a signpost. In 200 yards or so you bear left, climbing steeply to the buildings and going forward to a track. Keep climbing, enjoying superb views back across the Brede valley, and in a little over a quarter of a mile you reach a staggered footpath junction just before a pond to the left with farm paraphernalia around you; take the left path here and descend quite steeply, crossing the railway with care, to arrive back at the Brede by a footbridge*.

Just one of many beautiful old houses in Winchelsea, only a short distance from the river Brede.

Water, water everywhere - the river Brede between Winchelsea and Rye.

Your onward progress is now along the right bank of the Brede and you'll be able to follow this for most of the way to Winchelsea, the only landmark of note being a point where the river goes underneath the railway, your path actually crossing the line. Take care, as this is the main Ashford to Brighton line and trains pass along this stretch at some speed. Just under three miles from the footbridge at * you approach the steep hillside on which Winchelsea is built; a locked gate precludes further progress beside the river, so turn sharp right just before this gate, alongside a channel to a footpath sign at a little footbridge. Bear left across the footbridge and go forward, aiming for the base of the hillside, then as you reach it another footpath sign directs you left, bringing you to the A259. Turn left onto it then immediately left again onto the Winchelsea station road; follow the road to the bridge, cross the bridge then turn hard right on to a path that now follows the left bank of the Brede. It isn't a designated right of way, but at the time of writing there were no difficulties in accessing or following it. In just under half a mile you arrive at the A259; turn right to cross the bridge then bear almost immediately left onto Sea Road, signposted Winchelsea Beach. However by continuing a little way along the A259 and turning sharp left up the hill you'll reach the centre of the beautiful town of Winchelsea. The former town stood at shore level on a shingle spit to the seaward side of where the town is today. Following a storm in 1287 which washed most of the old town away, a new town was built, its grid pattern making it effectively England's first piece of town planning, and the grid pattern can still be seen today, with well-spaced-out houses, some of which are tile-hung and/or decorated with climbing roses and wisteria. Arguably Winchelsea's most interesting old building is St Thomas' Church with Sussex marbled effigies and canopies and pinnacled tombs that are some 700 years old. Also of note are the Armoury in Castle Street, which is of 14th century origin; the Court Hall, believed to date back to the first days of the "new" town and containing a museum; the 18th century New Inn; and three medieval gates, including Strand Gate which again dates back to the 14th century.

Returning to Sea Road, follow it just south of east for a little over half a mile until it swings sharply right. Leave the road here by following a lane eastwards (the same direction as the road had been following), soon swinging left (northwards); as the lane swings eastwards again, leave it by passing through a gate with a blue bridleway arrow sign. Initially it appears to be more of a private driveway, but by following it past a house, you're able to continue forward through another gate to arrive on the right bank of the Brede. Shortly after doing so, look to your right and you'll see the fine ruin of Camber Castle, built in 1539 on orders from Henry VIII as a defence against the French. At its peak of activity in 1542 it had a garrison of 42 men, but the main fortifications were demolished a century later. To continue to Rye, follow the river onwards, keeping to the right bank, only having to leave it to pass round the right-hand side of a large riverside house; once round the house, you bear left onto a signed bridleway which then returns to the Brede and hugs it all the way to the Rye Harbour road with its bridge over the Brede. Straight ahead you can see a basin and the point where the river is met by the Tillingham, but you need to turn left onto the road, then very shortly right to join the A259 which brings you to, and across, the Tillingham. Turn right and follow the greensward as far as you can, then at the end, turn right onto a path which passes to the left of a café and goes forward shortly to provide a view of the confluence of the Brede and Tillingham. It's possible to bear left here* and follow parallel with the Brede towards its confluence with the Rother, but the view to the water is obscured by private properties. So retrace your steps at *, climb up onto one of the hilltop vantage points in the town such as the Gun Garden or the Ypres Tower atop St Mary's Church, and view the meeting of the Brede and the Rother from above. The lovely town of Rye is more fully described in the chapter devoted to the East Sussex Rother.

The river Brede as it arrives in Rye - now wide enough to accommodate the Sea Breeze - and more.

CHRISTIANS RIVER / CUCKMERE RIVER

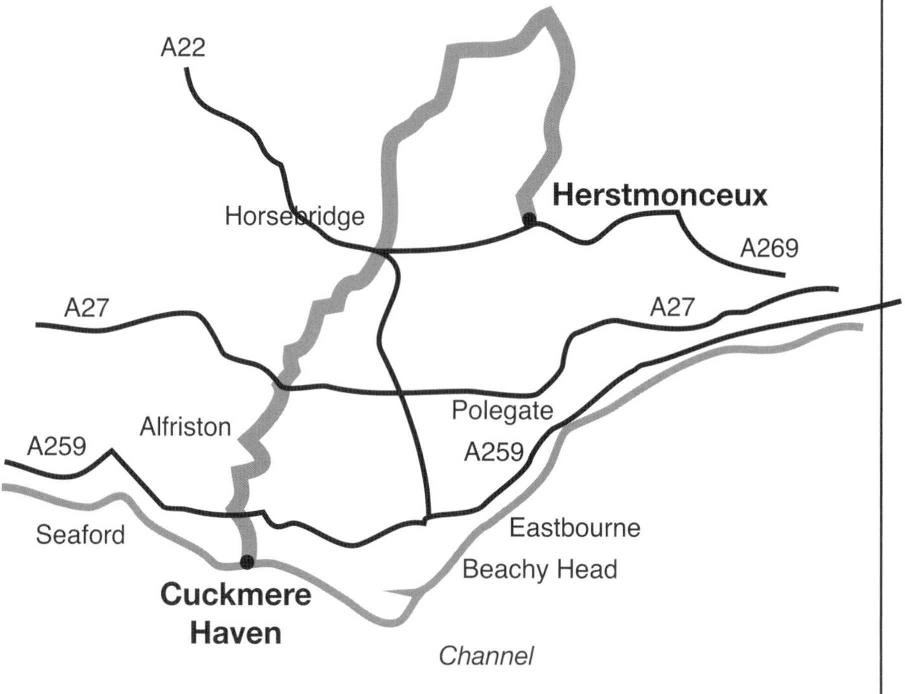

A22

Horsebridge

Herstmonceux

A269

A27

A27

A259

Alfriston

Polegate

A259

Seaford

Eastbourne

Beachy Head

Cuckmere Haven

Channel

CHRISTIANS RIVER / CUCKMERE RIVER

Length:	Approximately 23 miles.
Start:	Herstmonceux.
Finish:	Cuckmere Haven.
Public transport:	Regular buses to Herstmonceux from Eastbourne, Polegate and Hastings (not Sundays): regular buses linking Hailsham with Tunbridge Wells, Polegate, Eastbourne and Hastings (not Sundays); very regular and frequent buses to Seaford and Eastbourne from the Golden Galleon pub on the A259.
Refreshments:	Pubs and shops at Herstmonceux; pub at Cowbeech; pubs, shops and cafes at Hailsham; pub at Arlington; pubs, shops and cafes at Alfriston; pub and café at Litlington; pub at Cuckmere Haven by the A259.
Conditions:	This walk incorporates the best section of the little Christians River with one of the major rivers in Sussex. For much of the walk there are only intermittent riverside stretches, and although the scenery throughout is delightful, the walking is rather fiddly. However the journey climaxes in a quite superb walk along the more mature Cuckmere River culminating in the finest estuary in Sussex.

Following the river: Herstmonceux, the starting point of your walk, offers two superb visitor attractions, namely the grounds of its beautifully restored 15th century castle and the Observatory Science Centre, part of the former home of the Royal Greenwich Observatory and boasting over 100 exciting interactive exhibits. Note, however, that you will have to detour some way from the village centre to visit either of these. For your river walk, make for West End, the road for Cowbeech which heads north-westwards away from the main village street, but having joined West End turn almost immediately right into the metalled Bagham Lane, and follow it to just short of the buildings of the farms of Wenhurst and Nunningham. A footpath sign directs you round the left side of the buildings. Beyond them, you proceed north-eastwards, a signpost directing you initially, and follow the stiles through the fields, although be warned that signposting is

Time for reflection - a lovely spot beside Christians River near Herstmonceux.

poor and the path is very indistinct on the ground. Don't be tempted along a track that runs initially parallel with the north-easterly route, but then disappears away to your right. Continuing to aim for the stiles and heading north-eastwards, pass directly under the pylons and proceed downhill, crossing over a small footbridge then – once on the valley bottom – making for a more substantial footbridge over Pebsham Stream. Beyond this footbridge, bear left and continue along an obvious marked path which keeps the stream to the left, firstly through woodland then through meadows. Again just follow the stiles, in due course arriving at the metalled Chilsham Lane, onto which you turn right and which you then follow uphill to a T-junction. Turn right and pass the Nonconformist chapel, then immediately past the chapel turn left onto a path heading just north of east then swinging east, heading through a field. Don't be tempted to follow it round to the left; the correct line, again very unclear on the ground, is to the right of the cluster of vegetation you soon reach in the field, aiming in fact for a single very conspicuous tree. Go forward, losing only a little height, to the woodland which should be immediately ahead of you, and aiming for the left corner, enter it and pass down steeply through a gully to reach another road. Turn left onto the road and walk downhill until you reach the valley bottom, the bridge over Christians River now just ahead of you.

Just short of the bridge, turn left into the meadow, heading north through the meadow and keeping the river immediately to your right. You now enjoy a superb walk along an obvious path on the left bank of the river, passing Water Mill Farm and Great Buckstepe Farm; immediately to your left, in front of the farms, are quite delightful lakes, creating what must be one of the most unsung beauty spots in East Sussex, the tranquillity palpable, the woodland and meadow surroundings quite breathtaking. Christians River, with its brown waters, is a strange animal, in some places stagnant-looking and in others active and babbling. A little way beyond the second farm, the path swings left, away from the river, but as it does so you're now able to join a path which follows the right bank of the river; initially this proceeds in the shade of trees along the valley bottom with the ground rising steeply to the right, but when the wider path swings away to the right, steeply uphill, you keep to the path closest to the river. You're forced to rise gently but then drop down again to enter a thick wood, and you can now enjoy quite superb walking in beautiful countryside, especially in spring when the wood is carpeted with bluebells. You proceed through the wood, the river still close by you to the left, but all too soon your path is forced away from the river and rises to meet what looks like a dead end* just short of a fence. It was at the time of writing just possible to bear left and squeeze alongside the fence, negotiating some unpleasant bramble bushes and crossing over a low wooden fence to the right of a locked gate, going forward to a track which passes through a gate and the Little Buckstepe farmhouse to arrive at the road+. If the brambles prove too much, you can retrace your steps from * to arrive shortly at a path going off to the left; follow this clear path through the woods to emerge at a gate into a field, and go straight ahead, aiming for the gate at the other end. This may be tied up but the wooden fence to the right of it can fairly easily be negotiated. If you're uneasy about either alternative, seek permission as there appears to be no other convenient means of exiting from here, and the preceding walk is too good to miss. Having negotiated the wooden fence you immediately turn left onto a lane which proceeds uphill to a large house and a driveway which in turn brings you to the road; turn left along the road to arrive at + above. Now both routes proceed south-westwards along the road, passing over Christians River for the last time, then having bidden farewell to it, you head for the Cuckmere!

At the road junction that shortly follows, bear right and continue along the road uphill to a T-junction; turn right along the road and in just under half a mile, take the next road turning on the left. Follow this road to Iwood Place Farm, the first farm you come to on the right. Just beyond the farm, turn right onto a (plinth) signed path, at first going parallel with the road then striking out just west of south, aiming for the right-hand side of the woods ahead and avoiding temptation to head for the buildings of Egypt Farm that are directly south of you here. As you approach the right-hand side of the woods, aim for and cross the stile then turn right onto a farm lane which almost immediately swings left to reach the Batsford Farm House, a superb timber-framed building. Bear to the right of the house and reach a stile, with a footpath sign pointing half right. In fact you bear left here (no signpost at the time of writing but still a right of way), along the left edge of the field and aiming for a gate; pass through it and now descend south-westwards, aiming for thick woodland and a line of pylons ahead of you, the path faint but just about discernible on the ground. As you approach the valley bottom, aim for the footbridge which you cross, directly under the pylons, then use the steps to climb up through the charming Clippenham Woods to emerge at a field. Go forward through the field in the same direction, heading for the Clippenham Farm buildings, then join a track through the farm and continue along it to reach the road. Turn right onto the road which soon bends right to reach the hamlet of Foul Mile. Look out soon after the right bend for the house called Southfields on the left; immediately beyond it is a gate which you pass through to join a footpath, shortly signed, along the left-hand edge of the field ahead, still going south-westwards. Again the path is indistinct on the ground, but ahead of you is the mass of trees of Gutter Wood, and you follow immediately to the right of the trees. Soon a footpath sign reassures you, and you now follow the signs and the stiles, shortly entering the wood and following a very thin path. Emerging from the wood, you enter an area of marsh with houses ahead; look for the stile to your half-left which you cross, then proceed diagonally through the field, keeping to the left of the house at the top left-hand edge of the field. As you approach the house you see and join a clear path running past the house to arrive at the road. By turning left here you soon reach Cowbeech, which has a delightful pub, but to continue the walk, turn right onto the tarmac, following it for a few hundred yards down to a rather ugly waterworks. Just beyond the waterworks is a bridge crossing of a stream which is in fact the infant Cuckmere. Now retrace your steps past the waterworks, and turn right onto a path that goes off to the right via a stile just before the turning to Blackford Farm, following this path westwards. The Cuckmere is initially a little way across the overgrown meadow to the right, but soon you come to a footbridge over the Cuckmere, which has now swung sharply in from the

Rural idyll - one of the picturesque lakes beside which Christians River flows, complete with beautiful lakeside house.

right. Here you veer from south-westwards to north-westwards, and begin your riverside walk proper. For the next few miles you'll keep the Cuckmere to your left.

Keep walking along the signed path across fields, with the modest Cuckmere meandering very pleasantly to your left in the shade of woodland. The river, and your parallel path, now veers from north-westwards to westwards, passing to the south of Knightsbridge Farm to arrive at a road crossing. Cross the road and bear right, almost immediately arriving at a signed path which you now follow fractionally north of west, with the river still to your left. Soon the river, and your path, swing south-westwards and you proceed to enjoy a really easy, relaxing and straightforward walk along a clear path with rolling hills rising up on each side, the meadows and hillsides dotted with trees. It's lovely unspoilt walking, and soon there's another piece of interest to your right, namely the old Eridge-Polegate railway line. You keep walking with the river to your left and the old railway to your right, and as you do so, look out for a stone overbridge across the old railway; work your way round to the left of this, to reach a grassy track which is carried by this overbridge. Follow the track over the bridge and walk westwards, temporarily away from the river, to arrive shortly at a footpath crossroads. Turn left at this junction and proceed south-westwards, keeping a hedge to your right, then pass a pond which is on your right, and swing more obviously southwards to reach a T-junction with a road. Turn left and come to a crossing of the Cuckmere, noting a particularly lovely watermill at this point.

Beyond the watermill, turn right up the slipway to join the old railway which you follow southwards to an overbridge, immediately beyond which you turn right up another slipway leading to a road. Turn left to follow it, with the buildings and church tower of Hellingly straight ahead, then immediately before a bridge over the Cuckmere, turn left onto the signed Wealdway path. You will see a lot of the Wealdway in the coming miles; the Wealdway itself is an 82-mile walk from Gravesend in Kent to Beachy Head near Eastbourne, running via the North Downs, the Weald and the South Downs. With the Cuckmere to your right, you proceed along the clear path, beside the ponds and buildings of Horselunges Manor. Observing the Wealdway signposts, you keep walking, the Cuckmere to your right, along the clear path towards the vast and now rather unsightly pile that is Upper Horsebridge Mill. You pass the mill and go forward through a more open area to reach the busy A271 road which you cross straight over, and follow the road signposted Hailsham. Shortly turn right along Anglesey Avenue and then right again into Sheppey Walk, which you follow round to the left, looking for number 11. If you wished, instead of turning right along Anglesey Avenue, you could carry on into Hailsham. Its High Street has a number of good Georgian buildings, and the fine church of St Mary, which boasts a particularly fine west tower of flint and stone chequer in Perpendicular style. In the last century, Hailsham's rope factory had the dubious privilege of supplying the cords used in prisons for executions.

Returning to the route, look for a narrow path and Wealdway marker just to the left of number 11 Sheppey Walk, then follow this path which heads south-westwards, keeping the housing estate immediately to your left. You cross a stream then, as directed, strike out more firmly south-westwards, aiming for the right of the farm buildings ahead. The noise of the A22 traffic is very obvious here. As you approach the farm buildings, you'll see an obvious track passing immediately to the right of them; now follow the track, turning right at the T-junction onto a road which almost at once takes you to the A22. Cross with great care, then turn right and look for the signed Wealdway path going off to the left. For the next mile or so, the Cuckmere is out of sight to the right, although there are occasional glimpses of the valley bottom as you walk. Your route soon swings left, passing the left-hand side of a patch of woodland, and you must now follow the Wealdway signs carefully, as the next section of path is unclear on the ground. Shortly beyond the wood it veers sharply to the right to pass to the left of a pond, then left, right again to another pond, and left again, heading downhill to a marshy area, crossing a stile in a fence and then swinging westwards through some trees to enter a wide field. The path proceeds through the middle of the field, rising gently, then at the far end turns right to continue between two areas of woodland, and swings left to cross the Cuckmere. Almost immediately beyond the bridge the Wealdway is signposted right, between electric fences with farm buildings to the left, rising slightly. Shortly you reach a junction of paths; the Wealdway bears right towards Upper Dicker, but you take the left path along the left-hand edge of a field to arrive at a road junction.

Turn left here and follow the road downhill, passing the main entrance to the

An unusual bridge over Christians River, one of the more modest "name" rivers in Sussex.

magnificent house and gardens of Michelham Priory. The Augustinian priory, built on the site of a Norman manor house, dates back to 1229 and was dissolved in 1536 during the reign of Henry VIII; apart from a 14th century gatehouse, the later stonework of a Tudor farmhouse masks what survives of the original priory. Of particular interest are the Tudor rooms, furnished with an impeccably presented collection of Dutch paintings and Flemish tapestries and Old English furniture, the restored watermill once used by the monks, and some magnificent gardens. You cross back over the Cuckmere, and very shortly you turn right onto a signed field path, skirting the right hand side of an area of woodland. When the woodland peters out on your left, continue along the field edge, swinging round to the right and then, at the far corner, swinging left. Here you're briefly reunited with the Cuckmere which, in the shade of trees, looks particularly attractive just here. Follow the path carefully along the right-hand edge of a field, between electric fences, then as the river veers away to the right, you bear slightly left with the path, passing through a very pretty patch of woodland and emerging into a field. Now the going becomes straightforward as your path, which is clearly defined, rises and stays above the valley floor along the left-hand field edge. It swings a little to the right to enter a plantation, passing underneath a line of pylons, then bears left to leave the plantation and pass through a field, going forward to a T-junction with a farm track. Turn right onto this track, passing the buildings of Raylands Farm which are to your left. Beyond the farm buildings, the track narrows; you pass under the pylons again and

Christians River as it flows through beautiful bluebell woods, a riot of colour in spring.

soon turn left onto a signed footpath, now reunited with the Wealdway.
The next section is delightful; the path, clearly defined, proceeds initially southwards then just west of south, with the Cuckmere easily visible to the right, and the spire of Arlington Church providing an obvious landmark straight ahead. Aim for the church, the path in fact veering to the left of it, although you may wish to detour to visit it. The flint-built church of St Pancras dates back to Saxon times, with one of the existing windows obviously Saxon in origin, and contains an Anglo-Saxon nave, a Norman north chapel, and remains of medieval wall paintings. Passing through the churchyard, you reach a T-junction with a road. Turn right onto the road and, when it ends, continue along an obvious signed path which proceeds south-westwards, keeping the Cuckmere to your right with the Arlington Reservoir, which supplies water to Eastbourne, just beyond. You reach a T-junction with a metalled drive that services the workings close to the reservoir; turn right onto the drive which brings you to a T-junction with a minor road, just beside a bridge over the Cuckmere, then cross the bridge onto a signed path, still on the Wealdway, which proceeds initially beside the river. It's nice to have some riverside walking again, serving as a good appetiser for what is to come. Disappointingly, you're forced to swing left, away from the river, uphill beside a small tributary stream, then left along a clear path that strikes out in a south-westerly direction. Initially the Cuckmere is quite easily discernible, but as the river swings westwards you lose sight of it. You carefully cross over the Lewes-Hastings railway, then continue south-westwards

One of many fine manmade riverside features in Sussex - a weir on the Cuckmere near Hellingly.

along the Wealdway, and, keeping to the path, swing south-eastwards through farmland before veering south-westwards again to arrive at the A27 trunk road.

Cross straight over the A27, again taking great care, and proceed along the lane, soon reaching large houses on the right and left. Look out for a signed bridleway to Alfriston on the right, and follow it downhill to a footpath junction, with one path going off hard left and another, which you take, veering more gently to the left. Your path, hidden from the Cuckmere valley by the raised ruin of Burlough Castle, rises then descends gently to meet a road which you join, proceeding in the same direction. Follow the

The Cuckmere estuary at Cuckmere Haven, one of the loveliest riverside scenes in Sussex.

road, back within sight of the river, until you reach a junction with a road going off to the right; turn right onto this road and shortly you reach a bridge over the Cuckmere. Now at last the true riverside walking begins, and you're in fact spoilt for choice, with either riverbank available as you turn left off the road to begin your continuous walk by the river. Soon you reach the lovely village of Alfriston, where there's another bridge; if you have chosen the left bank to reach it, you'll need to cross the bridge to access the village. Arguably the grandest building in Alfriston is its 14th century church in a beautiful setting between the river and a large green; described as the "cathedral of the South Downs," it has unusual stonework of small, square, knapped flints. Its High Street contains many medieval buildings, and boasts a mixture of styles including tile-hanging, weatherboarding and brick and timber. The Star boasts ceiling timbers decorated with carved animals, and on the street corner beside the Star is a large red lion which is in fact the figurehead of a 17th century Dutch ship. On the edge of the green is the 14th century Clergy House, the first building bought by the National Trust. Beyond Alfriston you now enjoy three magnificent miles of riverside walking, following well-defined paths on either side; notice how initially the river is still quite narrow but as you progress it widens dramatically, with the scenery changing constantly and the water meadows immediately beside you complemented by splendid downland hills. The next village is at Litlington, a mile or so downstream, and again a footbridge is available in order to access the village from the right bank, or simply give you a chance to swap banks. Here the valley narrows, hemmed in by spurs of the Downs on either side; it is a very unspoilt village, boasting a pretty church with white weatherboarding immediately below its spire and, inside, a Norman nave and chancel. Delightful walking continues as you walk on to the A259, and you may be entertained by hang-gliders launching from the top of the steep slopes immediately to the right of the river. You may also receive inquisitive stares from the many cows which frequent the banks.

At length you arrive at the A259 by the Golden Galleon pub, and you have a choice of route to the sea. This final section of the Cuckmere is marked by spectacular meanders; the mouth of the Cuckmere drifted east because of encroachments of the shingle beach, and in order to prevent flooding, a new cut was opened in 1846. You may choose to follow either the cut or the "old" river route, which obviously is a lot longer. The **quicker**

route, beside the cut, goes straight across the road, and onto a path passing to the left of the Golden Galleon pub and proceeding resolutely along the right bank of the cut as far as its mouth at the beach; look out for the old coastguard cottages to your right, and the fine views of Seaford Head above. Having arrived at the beach, just retrace your steps to the Golden Galleon where there are buses to Seaford, Brighton and Eastbourne. The **more spectacular** route bears left alongside the A259 to a visitor centre, which provides a superb insight into the wildlife of the Cuckmere valley and the nearby cliffs. Look out more or less opposite the visitor

The Cuckmere arrives at the sea, flanked on one side by the coastguard cottages, and on the other by the Seven Sisters.

centre for a metalled track leaving the A259 and heading seawards, accessed by a gate, then proceed along this excellent track towards the sea, keeping the meandering "original" Cuckmere to your right. There are lovely views from here across the valley, known as Cuckmere Haven; it is the only river valley in Sussex to provide wildfowl with a natural merging of meadow marsh, saltings and wild seashore. The area attracts a huge variety of wildlife including ducks and waders such as the coot, mallard, moorhen, shelduck, dunlin, redshank and ringed plover, while other birds you may see include the curlew, peregrine falcon, hen harrier, yellow wagtail, sandpiper and yellowhammer. After about half a mile, the path swings quite sharply left, away from the valley, but rather than taking this left turn you bear right onto a path signposted SEVEN SISTERS CLIFFS/THE BEACH. You could choose to continue on to the beach, and then return to the A259, but a spectacular alternative, and a really fine climax to your riverside ramble, would be to follow the signposts directing you up onto the Seven Sisters cliffs and enjoy fantastic views across Cuckmere Haven to Seaford Head. If you felt really energetic you could keep walking along the Seven Sisters but if you feel you've had enough walking, retrace your steps to the A259 for bus services as indicated above.

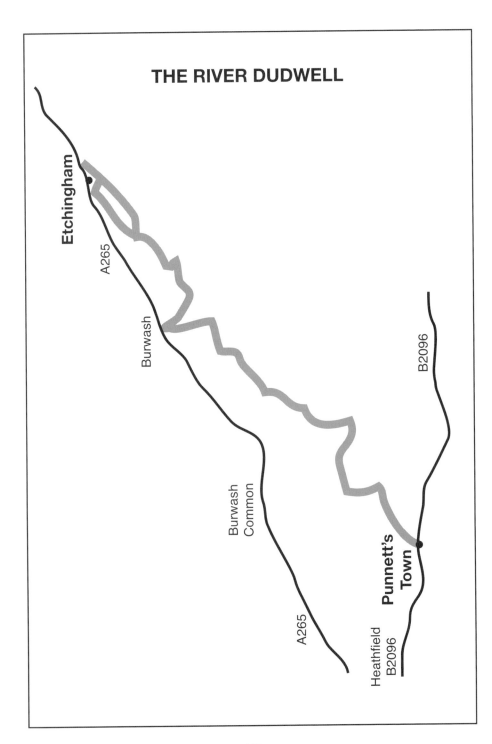

THE RIVER DUDWELL

Etchingham

A265

Burwash

Burwash
Common

A265

Heathfield
B2096

Punnett's
Town

B2096

THE RIVER DUDWELL

Length:	7 miles.
Start:	Punnetts Town.
Finish:	Etchingham.
Public transport:	Regular buses to Heathfield from Eastbourne, Polegate and Tunbridge Wells (not Sundays); infrequent buses linking Burwash with both Heathfield and Etchingham (not Sundays); regular trains from Etchingham to Hastings, Tunbridge Wells and London Charing Cross.
Refreshments:	Pubs, cafes and shops at Heathfield and Burwash; pub and shop at Etchingham.
Conditions:	Delightful walking in extremely attractive Wealden scenery, with the bonus of one of the prettiest villages in England. Be warned, though, that for a river walk, there is a significant amount of up-and-down work.

Following the river: A logistical difficulty presents itself at the very start of this walk, in that although the walk itself begins at Punnett's Town, there is no regular bus service to this village. Unless you opt for a taxi, it's best to get a bus to the Mutton Hall district of Heathfield; the Eastbourne-Tunbridge Wells service stops at the junction of Tower Street and the A265 Mutton Hall Hill. Having left the bus, follow the A265 eastwards then shortly branch south-eastwards onto the B2096 and follow this for 2 miles to Punnett's Town.

Golden Gate Bridge it ain't - the modest path crossings of the river Dudwell near its source.

Bateman's, the sometime home of Rudyard Kipling, close to the bank of the river Dudwell.

Fortunately there is a pavement all the way along, so the going is not too disagreeable. At Punnett's Town there are two big road junctions in the village centre; you leave the main road at the second, turning left into North Street then immediately right into Forest Lane. Follow the lane past Watkins Farmhouse, then continue along the lane eastwards, soon reaching an area of woodland. Immediately you reach the woods, bear left onto a path here, and follow it steeply downhill to reach a bridge over the Dudwell, a mile or so downstream of its source. Cross the bridge, bear right and follow a very rough path through trees, emerging at a gate which you go through and enter very pleasant meadows with the ground rising to the left. Continue beside the river through the meadow, arriving at a footbridge and a gate; pass through the gate and cross the bridge, bear round to the left, then at a break in woodland you turn left again, aiming for a newer wooden footbridge. Don't cross it but go forward into another large field, rising to pass between small ponds, continuing over the field and keeping the river below you to left. Unfortunately a tributary stream blocks your path, so on reaching the fencing in front of it you bear right and rise, going slightly back on yourself, and aiming just to the left of the prominent building in the field on the hillside; here, you pick up a signed footpath, going forward through a rough area and heading towards a fine oast house. Shortly a wider path comes in from the right, and you continue along a clear track past the oast house, veering left.

The firm track quickly goes away to the right but the signed path goes up steeply through the woods. Soon there's a signed crossroads of paths at which you turn left, and you now follow a well waymarked path through the woods, emerging into field high above the Dudwell valley, enjoying really lovely views to the valley. Follow the signed path along the hillside, rising slightly then meeting with a path coming in from the right and descending into the valley, with excellent views throughout. You drop down to the road just south of Willingford Bridge, crossing straight over the road onto a signed path which climbs north-eastwards away from the road, keeping the river to the left. In delightful surroundings the path continues through a field, then suddenly the ground seems to fall away and you drop steeply to reach the river again. Keeping the river to your left you go forward to the grounds of Bateman's; following round the left-hand edge of a pond, you arrive at a lane onto which you turn left, passing Bateman's and crossing the river. Bateman's, a fine 17th century Restoration stone house, was the home of Rudyard Kipling from 1902 until his death in 1936. He wrote some of his greatest work here including Puck Of Pook's Hill. The house, which is owned by the National Trust, contains many memorabilia of Kipling's life. Just beyond Bateman's, take the first metalled road on right, Bateman's Lane, and follow it to a T-junction with Alley Road onto which you turn left, climbing steeply uphill along the road past the church to reach Burwash.

Burwash is one of the prettiest villages in Sussex and indeed in England. The main village street, built on a Wealden ridge, boasts an almost unbroken line of lovely old shops and houses, many of them tile-hung or weatherboarded and dating back to the 17th and 18th centuries. During the 18th century it was an important centre of the iron

Burwash, close to the river Dudwell, provides the one opportunity for refreshment en route for Etchingham for Dudwell-side pilgrims. This is the Lime Tree tea room in the picturesque village centre.

industry and in the parish church of St Bartholomew, which boasts a Norman tower and Early English chancel, is a 14th century iron tomb slab which is claimed to be one of the oldest of its kind in the country. To continue from Burwash, make your way back to the church and proceed to the east end of the churchyard to join a footpath which heads eastwards out of the churchyard, going forward to a field containing 2 benches. Watch for a narrow, unsigned and rather faint path leaving the "main" footpath here, and take it; it passes just in front of the brown bench and drops steeply down the hillside, aiming for a kissing gate. Go through the gate into a field, follow the right-hand field edge downhill towards the valley bottom, then bear a little left and arrive at (but do not cross) a footbridge. Now turn left to enjoy a very pleasant walk along the left bank of Dudwell, but all too soon you reach a hedge which bars further riverside progress; turn left to follow the right-hand field edge beside a hedge as far as a stile in the hedge to the right, go over the stile and head across the field as directed by the footpath sign, arriving back at the Dudwell again with a footbridge straight ahead. The surrounding scenery is more pastoral, and less wooded, and the hillsides are less steep than earlier in your walk. On arrival back at the Dudwell, don't cross the footbridge, but bear left to follow the bank of the river, pass a further footbridge, and go forward to yet one more footbridge with a big farm complex close by on the other side with the lovely name Grandturzel. Now head north-eastwards, left, away from river as indicated on the signpost, aiming for a cluster of buildings which make up the Borders Farm complex; keep heading north-eastwards, passing to the right-hand side of a large pond/gravel pit, then swing in a more easterly direction and aim now just to the right of the Borders buildings. After crossing

This delightful assembly of buildings including oast house is situated in the valley of the river Dudwell near Etchingham.

over a very decrepit stile and footbridge, you have a choice. You could decide to play safe by following the footpath signs left through the farm complex to arrive at a metalled minor road, turning right onto it and following it for half a mile or so to Etchingham, turning right at the T-junction with the A265 to reach the village street. However you could choose to be more adventurous, passing to the right of the Borders complex, dropping slightly and continuing through meadows to pick up the left bank of Dudwell again. Using this more adventurous route, you now continue along the left bank, negotiating a tributary crossing with low barbed wire and wooden stile; a few hundred yards beyond this crossing, the buildings of Etchingham now in view, you arrive at a footbridge over the river, gated on either side. Cross this bridge to join the right bank of Dudwell which you follow to arrive very shortly at Oxenbridge Lane onto which you turn left, going uphill to reach the village street and meet the safer route described above. Please note that this

Etchingham Church, close to the confluences of the river Dudwell and also the river Limden with the East Sussex Rother, and one of the most interesting village churches on any of the Sussex riverside routes.

riverside route from Borders is not a designated right of way and although there are no signs prohibiting access, and there are no obstructions which cannot reasonably be surmounted, you may wish to seek permission before embarking on it. Etchingham, with his very attractive old church, is described in the section devoted to the East Sussex Rother; the railway station is easily reached by following the main street (A265) past the church and bearing left onto the station approach road just before the level crossing. The Dudwell can be seen just to the right of the road as you proceed to the station approach road and its confluence with the Rother is just over the other side of the railway. You could if you wish bid a final farewell to it by going past the station approach road and just short of the level crossing, turning right onto the metalled Lundsford Farm approach road; shortly you reach a bridge over the Dudwell and can watch it disappear under the railway on its way to join the Rother. The station, with excellent rail links, is a natural as well as satisfying conclusion to your walk along one of the most unsung and underrated of the rivers of Sussex.

THE RIVER MEDWAY

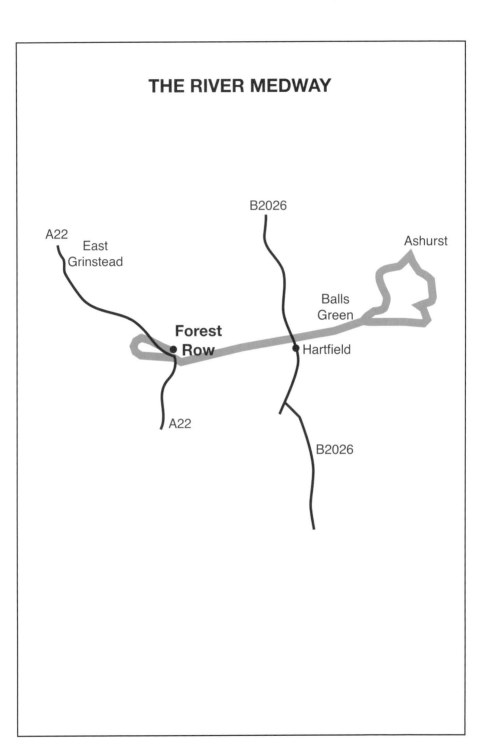

THE RIVER MEDWAY

Length:	Approximately 10 miles (add 1.5 miles for loop route at the start).
Start:	Forest Row.
Finish:	Hartfield.
Public transport:	Regular buses (not Sundays) running between East Grinstead and Tunbridge Wells via Forest Row, Hartfield and Groombridge.
Refreshments:	Shops, pubs and cafes in Forest Row; shops, pubs and café in Hartfield.
Conditions:	A very easy and rewarding walk through an area that is full of interest for the visitor.

Following the river: The Medway is essentially a Kent river, and most people if asked to visualise the Medway might think of its broad estuary crossed by the magnificent motorway and railway bridges at Rochester. However even the widest and most majestic rivers must have their beginnings, and the Medway's infant course is through north-east Sussex. It is hard to tell from OS maps exactly where it does start; a glance at the relevant maps would suggest that it rises between Crawley and East Grinstead, flows into Weir Wood Reservoir a few miles south of East Grinstead, and emerges from the reservoir a short way west of Forest Row. It's virtually impossible to follow the Medway upstream of the reservoir, and

Part of the Forest Way near Forest Row, in the valley of the river Medway.

109

The magnificent Brambletye ruins close to the banks of the river Medway.

therefore this walk starts at Forest Row and extends to Ashurst where it flows into Kent, concluding either at Hartfield or back at Forest Row, depending perhaps on time available.

Your walk starts from the junction of the A22 London to Eastbourne road with the B2110 Hartfield Road in the pleasant but unremarkable village of Forest Row. Before you start your walk "proper" to Groombridge there is the option of a preliminary "loop" route giving you the chance to see a little more of the Medway and the fine ruins of Brambletye. To do this, walk northwards beside the A22 briefly, cross over the river and turn left onto the signposted cycle route, the so called Forest Way, which climbs up to join the course of the old railway linking East Grinstead with Tunbridge Wells. Follow Forest Way along the course of the old railway to reach a crossing track signed Brambletye Crossing and turn left to join the crossing track. Proceed along it, initially southwards then swinging south-west, to pass the magnificent ruin of Brambletye, originally built by Sir Henry Compton in 1631. Continue beyond the ruins then as the path veers to the right, watch for a path going off to the left and take this left turn. Proceed along a good clear path to reach a bridge over the Medway, cross it and then turn immediately left onto a signed riverside path which provides good views to what is at this stage a modest river indeed. Follow the path which is very clearly defined, initially beside the river then uphill away from it, over two or three stiles and then downhill to arrive at Swans Ghyll, a road in a modern housing estate. Turn right onto the road and follow it uphill to a T-junction with Priory Road, turning left here to arrive at the A22/B2110 junction.

Whether you decided to do this loop route or not, you now walk alongside the A22 next to the village green a little north of the roundabout and turn right to walk immediately in front of the prominent Forest Row village hall, built in 1892, joining an obvious path eastwards. This crosses Hillside and Lower Road in quick succession, then bends a little south of east to proceed pleasantly through a small meadow, with the Medway close by to the left, to arrive at Station Road. Turn left onto this road, crossing a bridge over the Medway, then at the end of Station Road you reach a small industrial estate; look carefully for a "Forest Way" signpost directing you to the right, and go forward to rejoin Forest Way and the course of the old railway. The going is now extremely simple, as you follow Forest Way for four miles to Hartfield, keeping the Medway close by to your left.

Once you've left the houses of Forest Row behind, the landscape is predominantly wooded to your right, and more open to your left, allowing plenty of views to the Medway and its surrounding meadows. Look out for excellent views to the impressive Ashdown House to your left. Initially you head south-eastwards but then proceed resolutely north-eastwards in an almost dead straight line, until you arrive at a bridge under the B2026. Clear signposting leads you onto this road which takes you southwards (right) into the beautiful village of Hartfield. The village contains many delightful buildings, many of traditional weatherboarding and fronted by magnificently kept gardens, there is a most attractive church with a prominent spire and late 13th century features, and there are two pubs including the 16th century Hay Wagon. The

It's hard to believe that this, the river Medway, will mature into one of the great rivers of southern England.

village is perhaps best known for its association with A.A. Milne who lived just outside the village and who wrote the Winnie The Pooh stories to entertain his son Christopher Robin, and there's a shop-cum-tearoom in the village, Pooh Corner, which sells various Pooh memorabilia. Just a few miles south of Hartfield is the famous Poohsticks bridge which, although not crossing one of the watercourses described in this book, is certainly worth visiting if you have the time. Directions to the bridge can be obtained from the shop.

Retrace your steps to the Forest Way and keep walking eastwards along the footpath/cycleway, enjoying lovely views to the Medway to your left. At the next road crossing, at the rather inelegantly named hamlet Balls Green, leave the Forest Way and turn left to follow Beech Green Lane. Cross over the Medway, then shortly turn right onto a signed path. Follow it through the meadows, initially a little way from the river, then alongside it, then away from it again. When the river returns to the path-side again, there's a junction of paths, and here you fork right onto a permissive path which proceeds most attractively alongside the Medway. In due course you reach a footbridge, where sadly you must leave the river. Turn hard left to follow a path which goes to the left of the patch of trees and Hale Court Farm buildings, then as the path bends round to the left again, bear right onto a signed path which immediately crosses a stream and continues, tightly defined by fencing, round to the left then sharp right to reach a T-junction with another path. Bear right here, shortly reaching a T-junction with a metalled farm lane, turn left onto the lane and follow it uphill. As you climb there's a tall hedge to your

There is a close link between Hartfield, close to the river Medway, and Winnie the Pooh. Here is the mecca for all Pooh lovers! At the time of writing, it housed a tearoom with lots of tempting treats for walkers and would-be Poohsticks Bridge visitors.

right, but this ends and, as it does so, you can see the lane stretching ahead uphill with a little avenue of trees on the right. Don't continue alongside the avenue but turn right immediately beyond the hedge end down a path which was not signed at the time of writing. The path proceeds downhill through an orchard, and across a signed path junction to a footbridge just south-east of Blackham Court. Once over the bridge turn right onto a signed path which proceeds clearly across fields north-eastwards to arrive at the Medway again. Now follow the left bank of the Medway past the weir all the way to the road crossing, turn right onto the road and pass under the railway bridge, entering the village of Ashurst. This is as far as your Medway walk in Sussex can go, and you now need to return towards Forest Row. Turn right almost immediately onto the station approach road, go past the station then bear left, uphill, along a metalled lane. You reach a T-junction with a track and turn right onto it, passing Jessup's Farm; beyond the farm the path swings left and uphill again to reach a T-junction with another track. Turn right onto this track and follow it south-eastwards for a little over a quarter of a mile, enjoying lovely views to the Medway valley and surrounding countryside, until you reach and follow a signed path going off to the right. This proceeds steeply downhill and under the railway; immediately beyond the railway you bear left, and proceed south-westwards, the Medway just to your right, across a field to arrive at a path junction by a footbridge. Turn right to cross the bridge then bear immediately left onto a signed path across another field to arrive at the Forest Way embankment, a set of steps leading you up to the footpath/cycleway. Turn right onto the Forest Way and follow it westwards to Hartfield or Forest Row, with public transport links at both.

THE RIVER OUSE / IRON RIVER

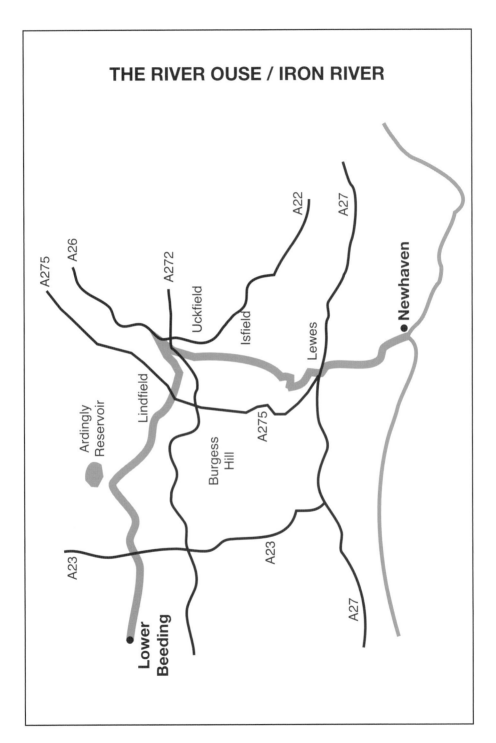

THE RIVER OUSE / IRON RIVER

Length:	Approximately 42 miles.(1 extra mile for detour to visit Iron River)
Start:	Lower Beeding.
Finish:	Newhaven.
Public transport:	Regular buses to Leonardslee (5 minutes walk from start of walk at Lower Beeding) serving Horsham, Henfield and Brighton: very frequent buses to Haywards Heath from Lindfield; regular buses from Haywards Heath to Uckfield via Newick (not Sundays); regular buses serving Isfield on the Tunbridge Wells-Lewes-Brighton route; regular trains from Lewes to Brighton, Eastbourne and London; regular trains serving Southease and Newhaven on the Brighton-Lewes-Seaford line; regular buses from Newhaven to Seaford and Brighton.
Refreshments:	Pub at Slaugham; pub and shops at Handcross; pub at Staplefield Common; pubs, shops and cafes at Lindfield; pub at Freshfield Bridge; pub and shop at Newick, slightly off route; pub and occasional café at Isfield; pub at Barcombe; pubs, shops and cafes at Lewes; pub at Rodmell; pubs, shops and cafes at Newhaven.
Conditions:	A magnificent and rewarding journey through lovely Wealden countryside with a mixture of meadows and woodlands, and passing a huge number of features of historical interest and beauty. A detour is possible onto the Iron River between Isfield and Barcombe.

Following the river: The Ouse competes with the Arun for the title of the most beautiful river in Sussex, and the most enjoyable and rewarding to follow. The river was once a very important means of communication, having been rendered navigable in the 19th century, with barges transporting goods and materials up the river until as comparatively recently as 1927. Moreover, the fast-flowing waters proved to be invaluable for milling, and at one time a series of mills along the river assisted in the manufacture of such diverse products as gunpowder, oil, paper and cloth.. Nowadays

Two views of the magnificent Ouse valley viaduct not far from Lindfield; an incredible feat of engineering, yet often passed unnoticed by passengers on the railway line over the viaduct.

the mills have all disappeared, and the only craft you'll see on the Ouse north of Newhaven are pleasure craft. The waters however continue to flow, growing from modest beginnings in tranquil Sussex countryside, and culminating in the wide and busy waters of Newhaven Harbour.

In view of the fact that there is a long-distance path known as the Sussex Ouse Valley Way, you might think that all you needed to do in order to trace the Ouse from source to sea was to follow this path. However, it's not as simple as that, for the first half of the Ouse Valley Way, as far as Vuggles Farm between Newick and Isfield, follows the bank of the river only very infrequently. In plotting a route for this book, I have tried to reach a compromise. As far as Lindfield, the trickle of water that is the river Ouse is so nondescript that walkers would be unlikely to find a trek along the bank particularly rewarding in any event, and I therefore advocate a straight overlap with the Ouse Valley Way to that point; the Way is often within sight of the river valley, passes several extremely interesting locations, and sees enough of the river to give you an insight into the maturing of the river almost from source. From Lindfield, however, as far as Vuggles Farm, "my" approved route deviates quite significantly from the Ouse Valley Way, as the riverside walking becomes not only eminently feasible but very rewarding and you'll miss little by preferring the riverside to the Way for this section. However many of the suggested deviations are along sections that aren't designated rights of way, and you should refer to my introductory notes on this subject.

Your journey starts at the bus stop by the entrance to Leonardslee Gardens on the A281. These beautiful gardens, started in 1801 by Charles Beauclerk, are set in a valley over 240 acres with seven lakes, mature trees, a collection of rhododendrons, some nearly 200 years old, azaleas, camellias, magnolias and over 400 types of alpine plant. To access the route itself, follow the Lower Beeding road (B2110) briefly, turning right along a signed driveway a few yards short of the village hall on the other side. Follow the driveway to the gateway to Keepers Cottage, here turning right onto a broad track and descending through the woods; observing the Ouse Valley Way signposts, you bear right twice in quick succession, crossing streams and then bearing left to follow a narrow path uphill into woodland. You arrive at a wire fence, bearing left and following the line of the fence to reach a stile. Cross the stile and leave the woodland, going straight ahead across a field, going over a stile to enter another field and going forward to arrive at a rough track. Turn left onto the track then bear right opposite some farm buildings after about a hundred yards; very soon you turn left and descend through woodland, bearing right at a fingerpost then almost immediately left to drop down to a footbridge over a stream. Beyond the stream you arrive at a wide track, turning right onto it, swinging left and ascending to a path junction. Ahead of you there are two tracks, and you need to take the right-hand one uphill; you arrive at another path junction in a clearing and again taking the right-hand of two paths, you go forward to reach a stile and lane. Turn left into the lane, passing Harvey's Farm and arriving at a T-junction with Warninglid Lane, where you turn right, then look out in about a hundred yards for a path leading off to the left. You follow this path, climbing through fields. This lovely path levels out and turns itself into a lane; continue along the lane past a couple of houses and at last get your first view of the Ouse as you descend to cross it by means of a footbridge, although it's a very modest strip of water indeed at this point.

Beyond the crossing you go forward to a road where you turn right, soon reaching Slaugham Furnace Pond to your left. Turn right at the crossroads, in due course reaching another bridge over the river; a short way beyond the bridge you turn left to go forward into a rather juicy area, using a modest bridge to cross the river again. Go on over a couple of stiles into a field on the right, then carry on along the left-hand field edge to cross a double stile and footbridge, entering another field which you cross diagonally right to reach yet another stile with woods to the right. Crossing another field, keeping the woods to your right, you reach a water treatment works, immediately beyond which you bear right, going over further stiles to enter a field, carrying on to reach a high wall to your right and going forward to the road. Turn right to follow the road into Slaugham, a very pretty village, with a particularly attractive Norman church that includes a 13th century tower and, in the south chapel, a superb monument to Richard Covert who died in 1579. When you reach the road junction opposite the church, take the road leading off to the left, and go straight on in the same direction beyond the white gateway along a lane which you follow, gradually gaining height. In just under a mile you reach a junction with a road onto which you turn left, then bear right at the T-junction, going forward into the village of Handcross and crossing over the A23. Once across the A23, you soon reach a road junction; turn right here and cross the road, looking out for a footpath sign by the Handcross village sign – the path entrance to the Nymans NT Woodlands – and following this path. Before doing so, you may wish to detour to visit Nymans gardens, begun in 1890 and boasting an historic collection of fine trees, shrubs and plants.

Your path drops quite steeply until, as you reach the foot of the hill, a path comes in from the left. Very shortly after this you bear left at a signpost marked "Long Walk" then keeping a stream to the left you carry on through delightful woodland including some splendid conifers. The track bears to the right and drops to a lake; turning right when you reach the lake you follow the lakeside path, going forward to a footbridge then ignoring the first path going to the left you continue to the next path junction where you fork left. Very shortly you bear left again, crossing a footbridge then going up some steps to enter a field. Now bear right and follow a metalled track close to the right-hand field edge, arriving at a cattle grid in the corner of the field. On the other side of the cattle grid, join the concrete lane, bearing right and following it first uphill and then downhill to arrive at the large village green of Staplefield Common and the Victory Inn, the name of which commemorates its hard-won conversion to a pub from grocer's shop. Go across the green, aiming for the cricket pavilion and crossing the road on the other side to take the signed track leading off in the same direction (do NOT go on up to the crossroads at the top end of the green). Follow the track to a stile, going on into a field and following the left-hand field edge, dropping to a kissing gate and a small enclosed garden area. Go ahead to a further stile, crossing it to enter a field, then turn right into the field, carrying right round the right-hand field edge to arrive at the Ouse again. Bear left to follow the Ouse.

Shortly you come to a wooden plank bridge over the river. Don't cross it but bear left away from the river, keeping to the right-hand field edge, soon turning right through a gap into a further field; here bear left and follow the left-hand field edge through two fields, going forward past a pill box – one of a number of World War 2 defensive constructions which can be seen beside the river today – to reach the B2114 road. Turn right to follow the road, crossing the still very modest Ouse, then go forward uphill along the road to the brow of the hill. You then bear left along a signed path through woods, descending gradually, reaching another gate, entering a field and going along the right-hand field edge to reach a gateway into further woods. Continue along an obvious track through the woods, arriving at a farm cottage and driveway, then join the driveway to arrive at Bigges Farm; maintaining the same general direction, pass the main farmhouse, keeping it immediately to your right as signposted, and join an enclosed path going forward to a stile and field. Keep now to the left-hand field edge, going on to a further field and then on in the same direction to reach a rough track. Turn left onto the track which veers firstly right then left, heading for a large farm ahead; about a hundred yards before the farm, you're signposted off the farm road where you bear left and then immediately right to follow a parallel track up through the farmyard and farm buildings. At the top bear right and go through the gate away from the farm eastwards along a lane which you follow for just over half a mile, arriving at a T-junction with another lane. Turn right here, dropping down to the B2036.

When you reach the B2036, turn left then almost immediately right to follow the Great Bentley Farm road; just before the gateway to the farmhouse, you turn left through a metal gate and go down some steps to a meadow. Now, keeping a stream to your left, you carry on ahead to cross a wooden footbridge over the Ouse. Bear half-right to cross a field, aiming for an oak tree and reaching a stile in the field corner; you go diagonally across the next field to the corner, going over two more stiles, aiming for farm buildings and a metal farm gate. Carry on through the farmyard, keeping the farmhouse to your right, then veer left along the farm road away from the farm. Very shortly turn right over a stile into a field, now heading for the Ouse Valley Viaduct which is undoubtedly one of the highlights of the walk. It was built in 1841 to carry the main London to Brighton railway across the Ouse valley; described as "one of the wonders of the Victorian age" it has 37 arches, stands 96ft high and over a quarter of a mile long, and required 11 million bricks, all of which were transported up the Ouse by barge! You pass over two stiles, go under the viaduct and go forward to reach the road onto which you turn right, then cross over the Ouse, and immediately turn left onto a signed path. Walk along this path beside the river, until you reach a wooden footbridge over it.

Now overlapping with the High Weald Landscape Trail, you turn hard right, away from the river, and cross the field aiming for the woods; you cross a stile and ascend through woodland, ignoring side tracks and going forward to the end of the wood at a farm gate. Continue in the same direction, crossing a bridge over a former link railway between the Bluebell Railway (see below) and the London-Brighton line. Go on to Rivers Farm, passing left of the main farmhouse then, maintaining the same direction, follow a line of oak trees to a plank bridge over a stream. You enter a field and carry on to a metal kissing gate, crossing another stream by a footbridge and going into a small wooded area. You pass to the right of a cottage ahead and carry on through the trees to arrive at the metalled Copyhold Lane; cross straight over, ascending through the woods on a clear path which emerges onto a golf course. You carry on ahead briefly along a path with a hedge on the right, then when the path veers left you go on to a footpath sign at the end of the hedge. Now you need to look out carefully half right across the fairway for another fingerpost in the trees separating fairways, and then follow the path as shown through the trees between the fairways, heading south-eastwards. You go forward to a driveway, with houses to your left, and arrive at a junction with another metalled road. Turn left onto the road – be careful, as this is a busy road – and follow it for about a quarter of a mile, turning right onto the Kenwards Farm lane. If you wanted another small "taste" of the Ouse, you could detour from the turn on to the Kenwards Farm lane, continuing along the main road past the Copyhold Lane junction and going downhill to the crossing of the Ouse at Lower Ryelands Bridge, but there's no riverside walk available

so retrace your steps and then follow the Kenwards Farm lane. In less than 200 yards turn right onto a rough track, going uphill, keeping the farm to the left and views to the Ouse valley beyond. You reach a junction of tracks and turn left, sticking to the main track, and dropping down into woodland. You then rise again, reaching a further path junction where you turn left onto an enclosed footpath, with houses and gardens to your right and extensive views to the Ouse valley to your left. You arrive in a gravelled courtyard in which you bear right, then shortly left to arrive at the main street at Lindfield. Turn right to walk to the church lychgate. Lindfield, although effectively a suburb of Haywards Heath, is one of the prettiest villages in Sussex; owing its prosperity to traditional industries including paper, gloves and

A pretty bridge over the river Ouse near the viaduct, and the point where sadly the Ouse Valley Way has to forsake the riverbank for some miles.

candles, its main street boasts buildings with timber framing, tile hanging and elegant 18th century brickwork. Among the best buildings of Lindfield are the former Tiger Inn with its fine red brick façade and timber-framed sides, the timber-framed Old Place with its massive roof of local Horsham slate, the 18th century brick-built Lindfield Place, and the 14th century parish church with shingled spire.

From the lychgate, pass to the left of the church through the churchyard, going forward to a rough driveway. Turn right and follow this briefly then bear left down Church Close; when it veers to the right, go straight ahead on an enclosed path, emerging into open country and arriving at a path junction where you turn left and follow a clear path to a farm entrance. Go straight on along a signed path, following a left-hand field edge to arrive at the Ouse, then bear right to follow alongside the Ouse as far as the road at East Mascalls Bridge. You now have a choice between a rough route and an easy but less interesting road route. For the easy route, turn left (northwards) onto the road and follow it past Paxhill Park golf course (a footpath leading off to the right a little way past the clubhouse cuts a significant corner off this road) and then eastwards, continuing to a T-junction. Turn right here, descending to the Ouse at Freshfield Bridge. For the rough route you cross straight over the road at East Mascalls Bridge and join a path which although not a designated right of way is easily accessible and continues alongside the Ouse, keeping it to the left. Initially your walk is through lovely meadows then enters woodland, the path however remaining clearly defined, albeit slippery and muddy after rain. Keeping the Ouse immediately to your left, and in the shade of trees, you proceed most pleasantly; in due course you arrive at a very narrow stream crossing with two parallel logs forming a crude bridge, and unless you're an experienced tightrope walker, you'll need to manoeuvre your way across the log on your backside, or wade the stream which although not deep will test the waterproof qualities of your boots! Beyond the crossing, rise quite steeply to get clear of the trees, and continue parallel with the Ouse but some way above it. You pass round the edge of the Scaynes Hill Water Treatment Works then bear half-left through rough grass, downhill again towards the river, to pick up a wider riverside path much loved by bikers, if the tracks in the mud are anything to go by. Follow this path beside the river, observing a delightful weir to your left, to reach a T-junction with the waterworks approach road, then turn left to follow the road, arriving at a T-junction with a public road immediately opposite the the Sloop Inn. This is one of only a couple of inns that actually lie on the bank of the Ouse, Freshfield Bridge lying immediately beyond to the left, and popular with the bargees in the period between the opening of the adjacent Freshfield Lock in 1799 and its closure in 1868, the year in which operations on the so-called "Upper Navigation" of the Ouse came to an end.

Unfortunately there is no through access beside the river from Freshfield Bridge as far as your next staging post, Sheffield Park. However, it is possible for you to walk some of the way to Sheffield Park beside the river, although it isn't a designated right of way; to do this, enter the farmyard on the north side of Freshfield Bridge, directly across the river from the Sloop Inn, and go forward into fields. You are now able to walk beside the Ouse through fields eastwards towards Sheffield Park. It is lovely walking, with picturesque woodland immediately on the other side of the river, but the way forward is blocked by a tributary stream so retrace your steps to Freshfield Bridge and the adjacent Sloop Inn. Make your way southwards from the inn along the road, and going forward to the turning to Bacon Wish and Field Cottage, now back on the Ouse Valley Way. Turn left to follow this driveway past these houses, crossing a stile and going on to a second stile on the right. Bear right here to follow the Ouse Valley Way uphill through the trees, reaching a third, very low stile. Cross this and keep on through the trees, climbing quite steeply, emerging into a field; you cross the centre of the field towards the woods, bearing left as signposted to pass a small pond which is to your right in the corner of the woodland. Carry on ahead over the field to a stile, crossing here from West to East Sussex, and go over it, along a path going in the same direction, now in Wapsbourne Wood. Keep along here for nearly half a mile to a T-junction, turning right here then almost immediately left, descending to arrive at a footbridge and then stile at the edge of a field. Turn left to follow the field edge and continue through the field, keeping the woods to your left, arriving at a stile to the right of a house. You cross the stile into a fenced grassy area, then turn right onto a driveway past tennis courts that are to your left. Shortly you get within sight of the very attractive Wapsbourne House, swinging left and following the driveway on to the A275, bearing left just before it onto a path that goes downhill parallel with the road. You then follow alongside the road as far as

An unspoilt spot on the river Ouse near Isfield.

the entrance to Sheffield Park Station; a riverside walk is available by turning left onto the station approach and then immediately right, downhill, to arrive at the river, and you are able to follow the river for about 250 yards as far as the bridge before being forced back to the road.

It is worth giving up at least half a day of your Ouse pilgrimage to enjoy what Sheffield Park has to offer. It boasts superb gardens adjacent to the 18th century Sheffield Park House which was built for the 1st Earl of Sheffield by James Wyatt; the 120-acre landscaped garden and arboretum with its 2 lakes was created by Capability Brown for the Earl of Sheffield in 1776. The station is the southern terminus of the Bluebell Railway, which is made up of part of a line which linked Lewes with East Grinstead. Opening in 1882, it closed in 1958, but almost immediately a preservation society was established, and the result was the steam railway that remains one of the most popular tourist attractions in Sussex. Even if you don't fancy a train ride, you can enjoy pottering around the station, which boasts pub/restaurant facilities and an excellent souvenir shop. From the station approach road, turn right and almost immediately left down the steps as signposted, still on the Ouse Valley Way, and you are now able to follow the Ouse for some time. You could follow beside it through the meadow as it describes an elaborate meander, but the grass is rough and lush, and you may prefer to stick to the main path and wait for the river to join you again. The path eventually bears right into the woods and you now go uphill through Rotherfield Wood, ignoring a crossing track. At the top you reach a T-junction with a road, where the Ouse Valley Way bears right, but you bear left along the road which you follow for nearly a mile, enjoying lovely views ahead to Fletching Church, and to the Ouse valley on your left. You pass some redbrick cottages, then drop down quite steeply to the river at Fletching Mill Bridge; just short of the bridge there is a gate and plinth with footpath sign to the right, and you follow the path which, clearly defined and marked, proceeds in a roughly south-westerly direction, the Ouse clearly visible to the left. Follow the path through some trees and under a line of pylons, and across an area of marshland where there are boards to ease your progress. You pass through another small wooded area to arrive at the edge of a very large field; turn left here to follow the field edge along a reasonably well-defined path albeit not a designated right of way. Continue along this path which swings to the right, keeping a fence to the left, and climb uphill, enjoying good views of the Ouse which can be seen to the left. Climb steeply, then, continuing to keep the fence to your left, swing sharply left and go forward to a clear track which you follow round the left hand side of Goldbridge Farm, and go on to reach the A272, crossing over with care. By turning right you soon reach Newick, with amenities including buses, but your route turns left and almost immediately right through a gate into a field.

Having entered the field, bear left and make your way along the field edge down to the river, observing a fine weir and Gold Bridge – where the Ouse passes under the A272 – to your left. Now follow an obvious and very attractive path along the Ouse, which again isn't a designated right of way, although access was no problem at the time of writing. Keep walking alongside the river until you are forced away from it by a crossing stream; bear right then left to cross the stream by means of a metalled gated farm bridge, then continue in the same direction – the Ouse now a little way away to your left – to arrive at a signed footpath pointing you left, picking up the path linking Newick and Sharpsbridge. Turn left here to enter a field, and follow the path along the left-hand field edge. Initially the Ouse is nearby to your left, separated from you by a strip of woodland, but soon you find yourself rising; continue to climb, all the time keeping the Ouse, and the intervening strip of woodland, as close as you can to your left, ignoring a tempting looking swing to the right. This is fantastic walking, arguably the best of your journey so far, with the Ouse clearly visible down to your left, and lovely views to the Sussex Downs on your right. Keeping the Ouse to your left, you now descend through an open field to arrive at the road.

Turn left onto the road and descend quite steeply to arrive at the river again at Sharp's Bridge, but just before the river crossing, turn right through a gate and enter the meadow beside the river. Again, this isn't a designated right of way, but you are in fact able to follow the river all the way to Vuggles Farm, keeping it to the left. It really is lovely walking, and access presents no apparent difficulty, with a crossing stream that is able to be negotiated by a narrow concrete bridge – not as primitive as the parallel logs near the Sloop Inn!! – and the odd stile at field boundaries as well. In due course you arrive at a line of fencing, with Vuggles Farm buildings immediately to your right, and turning right in front of the fencing, you are shortly reunited with the Ouse Valley Way. Turn left to follow the Way, an obvious path which continues to keep the Ouse to your left, a little way away initially but soon getting much closer and passing a magnificent waterfall for which a short detour is necessary. Shortly beyond the waterfall, you rise briefly to reach a track which you follow for a couple of hundred yards, then, continuing to keep the Ouse to your left, you turn left as signposted onto a riverside path through the meadows, going forward to White Bridge. Turn left to cross the bridge, then beyond the bridge bear right to rejoin the bank, but this time the left bank. By continuing along the track beyond the bridge you shortly reach Isfield with a really excellent bus service to Tunbridge Wells, Lewes and Brighton. It has a pretty church a little way to the north, in fact close to the east bank of the Ouse, containing tombs of the Shurley family, and the chapel still has 16th century linenfold panelling and pews. The most interesting aspect of Isfield's centre is its old railway station on the now defunct Lewes to Uckfield line. The line opened in 1858 and shut in 1969 but Isfield Station was restored, track was relaid, and trains began to run along a small stretch of line towards Uckfield. It continues to flourish today as the Lavender Line, after the coal merchants A.E. Lavender who used to operate from the station yard. The walk beside the Uck starts here (see below).

Back by the Ouse, you proceed most pleasantly along the left bank from White Bridge towards Barcombe Mills, enjoying very easy walking; you are on the Ouse Valley Way all the way to Barcombe Mills so if in doubt, follow the excellent signposting. Soon you pass under the bridge carrying the old Lewes-Uckfield line. *Immediately before the bridge there's a chance for you to visit one more "name" river in Sussex, namely Iron River which curiously starts and finishes its journey at the Ouse. I'm not sure it really is worth the detour but there are two circular walks you can do which will enable you to see a good part of it. The first involves turning left immediately before the old railway bridge and walking parallel with the old railway until you reach a little hump-backed footbridge over what is indeed Iron River. By crossing the bridge and turning left you can follow the right bank through a couple of fields but no more, as a tributary stream bars your way. However if rather than crossing the bridge you turn left onto the left bank of the stream, you can follow it all the way back to the Ouse again, a distance of about half a mile, simply having to leave the bank at one point to access a gate into the next field. Note however that it isn't a designated right of way, and the going is pretty rough, through long grassland. On return to the Ouse, proceed for a second time to the railway bridge.* Beyond the old railway bridge, go forward to the Anchor Inn which lies on the opposite bank; the inn was built in 1790 for the purpose of providing for those working the barges, and trade declined with the departure of the last barges in the 1860's, but it remains a very popular and beautifully situated country pub to this day. Immediately beyond the inn, there is a bridge over the Ouse which you cross. *Before doing so you could do another and rather easier circular detour to visit Iron River, following a signed footpath which proceeds north-eastwards from the Anchor, going almost, but not quite, back on yourself! It's a good path across the field which takes you to a gated bridge over the river, and by looking left you can see it passing underneath the old railway. You may content yourself with that and return the same way to the Anchor, but if you wish to follow Iron River a little more, retrace your steps briefly then turn left through the first gate into a field, giving you access to the right bank of Iron River as it heads southwards. It's good, easy walking, but almost too soon the river goes off and you find yourself being forced round to the right, now on the right bank of a tributary stream. Continue round the edge of the field to a gate, pass through it and proceed briefly to reach the Anchor, crossing the bridge here as stated.* Once over the bridge you now continue briefly along the right bank. Shortly the river divides, and you carry on beside the right (western) arm of the river, going forward onto a slightly raised path, passing a house that lies to the left among trees. Emerging into more open country, you arrive at a T-junction with a track. You turn right onto this track then shortly left as signposted over the western arm of the Ouse to join and follow its left bank; effectively you're now walking between the two arms, and delightful walking it is. Soon you cross another footbridge and continue along the left bank, with Barcombe Reservoir to your left. You cross a tributary stream soon after which the main Ouse goes slightly away to the right, but you continue beside a narrower channel which you will notice incorporates so-called "fish ladders," a reminder that this is a popular spot on the Ouse for fishing for sea trout. Continue forward to the fine old Pike's Bridge, grooves in the parapet of which were cut by ropes that were used to haul barges. At Pike's Bridge turn right to join a narrow metalled lane, crossing straight over Pike's Bridge itself and continuing along the road over the main Ouse channel, perhaps pausing to be amused by the table of tolls that are still exhibited by the bridge. Beyond the bridge the lane swings sharp left and goes forward to a T-junction* with a busier road that links the main A26 with Barcombe Cross; almost immediately opposite is a gate which takes you into a field, and you could cross the field to gain access to the right bank of the Ouse. At the time of writing, although it is not a designated right of way, there was no indication that such access was forbidden. However, although you can continue to Hamsey, the next village, beside the river throughout, without having to surmount any obstructions, there is a notice as you emerge onto the road at Hamsey that there is no public access permitted onto the land on which you have just been walking! It must be a matter for your own conscience, but my advice is to seek permission as there is no sure indication as to what section or sections of this walk from Barcombe Mills to Hamsey might be treated as permissive. NEITHER MY PUBLISHERS NOR I CAN TAKE RESPONSIBILITY FOR ANY ADVERSE CONSEQUENCES TO YOU OF YOUR BEING CAUGHT TRESPASSING. If in doubt, play safe and follow the Ouse Valley Way. Both routes to Hamsey are described in the next paragraph.

The Ouse Valley Way route turns right at the T-junction starred above to follow the road. You pass Barcombe Mills old station, then as the road bears right and goes uphill you turn left over a stile into a field beside a pill box, then follow the left-hand field edge to a stile leading into a second field. You go ahead following the left-hand field edge to a third stile, then proceed to another stile and footbridge into rougher pasture, carrying on to a footbridge over a ditch. Very soon you cross the track of the old Lewes-East Grinstead line(see above) and reach a further stile that takes you into a big field, which you go over, aiming for a fingerpost to the left of the tree line, taking you to another big field. You cross this, aiming half-right towards a house; on reaching a fenced paddock you pass through a gate, aiming for a wooden gate and signpost, then bear left onto an enclosed footpath which comes out onto a drive leading to a house named Wychwood. The drive takes you to a lane providing easy access to the village of Barcombe to the right, with its prominent church. You cross the lane and enter a big field, following the right-hand field edge, then go through the gap into another big field; at the next boundary you cross a concrete bridge into a further field, aiming for the buildings of Cowlease Farm. You go past these buildings, joining a concrete track, then as the track bears right you carry on ahead on the grass to the right of houses, emerging into a field. You cross the middle of the field, keeping in the same direction, passing over a ditch into a further field, which you cross to reach a line of trees at the right-hand edge of the field. You go forward beside a ditch to a track, continuing ahead to arrive at a lane; turn left onto this lane, and follow it through the little village of Hamsey as far as a sharp right hand bend+. **The riverside route** passes through the gate opposite the T-junction starred above, goes down through the field to the riverbank and follows the bank initially. The way beside the bank is obstructed and you need to head for and go over a stile on the

Two views of the Ouse near Barcombe, combining the beauty of nature with the ingenuity and endeavour of man.

right which leads you onto the course of the old Lewes-Uckfield line; join the line, heading south-westwards, but in just a few yards you leave it and walk down to the riverbank. It's then possible for you to follow the riverbank all the way to Hamsey. It is lovely walking with the enticing prospect of the South Downs escarpment ahead; because of the meanders it's a longer walk than that taken by the Ouse Valley Way, but it is, I have to say, rather more enjoyable and certainly more satisfying. In due course the superbly sited hilltop Hamsey Church comes into view, and as it does so, look out for a pipe bridge over the river. At this bridge the main Ouse goes off to the left and you continue along a narrower, straighter cut to arrive at a gate that takes you to the lane and the point marked with a + above.

Now the going gets easier. Follow the lane from the bend, heading south-westwards. The road, running south-westwards from the point marked + above, very soon bears sharp right and you leave it here, following the signposted Ouse Valley Way south-westwards along the bank of the cut. In a little over a quarter of a mile the main channel of the Ouse merges with it, and you will now have the main Ouse for company throughout the rest of your walk! Continue briefly south-westwards along the right bank, going towards the bank of the main London-Lewes railway line – to your right is the point where the Lewes-Uckfield branch once left the main line – then, just short of the railway embankment, the river, and your riverbank path, swings south-eastwards. Now follow the right bank towards Lewes,passing through the outskirts of the town. In just under a mile you reach a footbridge which you cross, then, as signposted, bear immediately right onto a metalled path; this proceeds close to the left bank, then, beyond Tesco store, goes down to the water's edge and passes under a road bridge. Once under the bridge, you are directed left, away from the river, then shortly right, going forward past a car park along a narrow alley to arrive at the pretty High Street of the district of Cliffe. Turn right onto this street and pass the Harvey's Brewery which is to

The attractive Cliffe High Street, just across the river Ouse from Lewes.

your right, crossing the bridge over the Ouse; immediately in front of you is a modern precinct, and beyond this, and the main road, is the delightful old centre of Lewes. The county town of East Sussex, Lewes is built on a steep chalk promontory. Its most ancient surviving building is the remnant of the Norman castle, the most impressive aspect of which is the superb barbican which was added early in the 14th century. In due course, Lewes became the centre of what was a substantial agricultural district and enjoyed considerable prosperity. The main street is lined with splendid old timber-framed and brick-built town houses, and the Southover area is particularly rich in old town houses including the timber-framed Anne of Cleves House dating back to the start of the 16th century. It was as recently as 2000 that the Ouse in Lewes made national headline news, when, after weeks of heavy rain, it burst its banks and caused flooding which devastated nearby houses and businesses.

Having crossed the river you take the first left-hand turn into Railway Lane, keeping a food hall to your left, and soon there is a reassuring Sussex Ouse Valley Way signpost. Keep going, shortly being reunited with the water's edge, then continue along the embankment path, passing under the railway bridge and shortly under the A27 Lewes bypass. Now the going again becomes straightforward, with a clear embankment path on the right bank for the next 4 miles, and lovely downland views.. Near at hand, to your right just under a mile after crossing under the A27, is a distinctive hillock called Lower Rise, and about half a mile beyond that is quite an extravagant meander, with the Lewes-Newhaven railway very close on your left. Shortly beyond the meander is a path leading off to the right which gives easy access to the National Trust-owned Monk's House; it was here that the novelist Virginia Woolf had her country retreat between 1919 and 1941, when she tragically died by drowning herself in the Ouse. The riverside walk passes the bridge carrying the South Downs Way over the Ouse at Southease, but it's worth detouring a little away from the river here to view the lovely Norman church of St Peter at Southease, which has a stunning setting above a village green with a manor house behind. Although some Norman work remains, the most interesting features of the church are the Jacobean pulpit and the 15th century chancel arch of wood, lath and plaster. Continue on along the bank until you reach a signpost with yellow arrow directing you onto a path to the right, away from the bank. Follow this to a road onto which you turn left, now separated from the river by houses, and keep along the road for half a mile to Piddinghoe, bearing left onto the road towards the village church. Piddinghoe is a most attractive village of flint-built cottages grouped round two small greens, but it was once a busy workaday place with a forge and malthouse; bricks were manufactured here, and the quayside was used for unloading cargo well into the 20th century. The 12th century flint-built church, one of only 3 round-towered Norman churches in Sussex, is topped by a shingle spire with a golden fish-shaped weather vane. Bear left of the church to join a path that then rejoins the embankment, and you now follow this on to Newhaven, becoming much more aware of the more industrial and less pastoral surroundings. Soon you reach an arm of the river going off to the right, the path going with it; unfortunately you're forced away from this "arm," finding yourself on a path which arrives at an Ouse Valley Way fingerpost pointing left. Bear left along a metalled road, then immediately before the factory gates turn right up a narrow path which then swings left to arrive at a T-junction with a main road. Bear left along the footpath/cycle path, following it round, aiming for the big swing bridge over the Ouse, which is as close as you get to Newhaven. Previously, the town wasn't actually situated by the Ouse, the river arriving at the sea some miles to the east, near Seaford, but the Ouse changed course to arrive at the sea here, a Harbour Commission was formed in 1731, and by the middle of the 18th century ships of up to 150 tons were using it. In 1825 a Dieppe passenger service was developed, which continues to this day, and in both World Wars it served as an important supply base; in recent years, the leisure industry has grown in importance here, and the harbour now boasts a yacht marina. The town itself has an intricate street pattern and a steep High Street running up to the fine church of St Michael with unusual blue and white interior décor, a shingle spire, and Norman features. Another building of interest is the white-painted Bridge Hotel which dates back to 1623; Louis Philippe, having been deposed in 1848, stayed here after fleeing revolutionary France.

Don't go over the swing bridge but cross the road leading to the bridge, then turn first left onto a concrete road/cycle path signposted Newhaven Marina. This is fascinating walking, the Ouse so much more impressive than a few miles back. Pass through what is a complex of buildings and boatyards, heading for the marina, then at the RNLI shop bear right to head out of the complex (at the time of writing this area is being further developed, so watch for any re-routings of the public right of way through it). You emerge from the complex at a T-junction with Fort Road, where it's worth leaving the route to visit Newhaven Fort. This provides an opportunity to step back into wartime Britain and experience the sights, sounds and smells of the two World Wars. Audiovisual presentations and exhibits are set inside a fortification where massive walls, ramparts, gun emplacements and towers can still be seen; the museum is housed inside casemates which once served as living quarters for soldiers stationed there. The Ouse-side route turns left at the T-junction and follows the road beside the river, all the way to the mouth, and as you reach the mouth there's a grassy area to the left, providing fine views eastwards to Seaford Head. This is the end of your pilgrimage and all it remains for you to do now is to retrace your steps to the centre of Newhaven. Newhaven Town station, with regular rail services to Lewes and Brighton, is just a short way across the river via the swing bridge mentioned above, and is clearly signposted, or alternatively there is a very good bus service along the coast road from Newhaven to Brighton.

*The pretty church at Hamsey, beautifully situated on a hill
overlooking the river Ouse.*

THE RIVER ROTHER (EAST SUSSEX) /RIVER LIMDEN

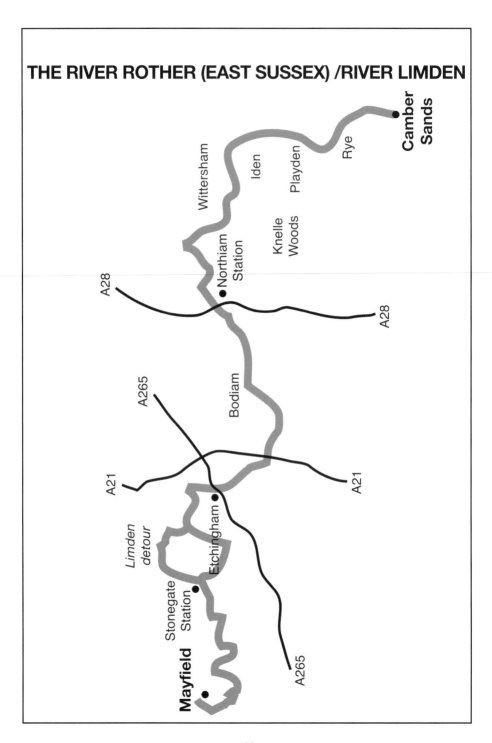

THE RIVER ROTHER (EAST SUSSEX) /RIVER LIMDEN

Length:	Approximately 30 miles (add extra 5 miles for Limden detour)
Start:	Mayfield.
Finish:	Camber Sands.
Public transport:	Regular buses serving Mayfield on the Tunbridge Wells-Heathfield-Polegate-Eastbourne run (not Sundays); regular trains serving Stonegate, Etchingham and Robertsbridge on the London(Charing Cross)-Tunbridge Wells-Hastings line; regular buses linking Newenden and Northiam with Tenterden, Hastings and Rye (not Sundays); regular trains serving Rye on the Brighton-Eastbourne-Hastings-Ashford line; regular buses linking Camber with Rye and Hastings.
Refreshments:	Pubs, shops and cafes at Mayfield; pubs, shops and café at Ticehurst (part of Limden detour); pub and shop at Etchingham; pubs and shops at Robertsbridge; pub at Salehurst; café at Bodiam; pub at Newenden: pub, café and shops at Northiam; pubs, cafes and shops at Rye.
Conditions:	The walk by the Rother is a walk of two halves. From the source to Robertsbridge the amount of riverside walking is sadly limited, progress can be fiddly, and the river itself is not a particularly attractive feature. From Robertsbridge, however, it is possible to follow the river almost all the way to the sea, often utilising not only existing rights of way but established long-distance paths, with straightforward and enjoyable walking virtually throughout. The Limden detour offers the opportunity to view a further Sussex river and a tributary of the Rother although frustratingly very little of the river itself is actually accessible.

Following the river: As is often the case with Sussex rivers, it is hard to ascertain where the East Sussex Rother actually begins, with maps of the area showing a number of watercourses coming together to form a single river which, from just south-east of Mayfield, is marked as the Rother. The Wealden village of Mayfield is therefore the most natural starting point. It has an exceptional variety of brick, sandstone and timbered houses; among its most noteworthy buildings is the oak-beamed Middle House, the 15th century sandstone gatehouse which guards the remains of what used to be a palace of the Archbishops of Canterbury, and the partially 13th century St Dunstan's Church with Jacobean pulpit and some excellent stone carvings. Starting from Middle House in the village centre, walk down the High Street, forking left into West Street and continuing down this street to a T-junction with another road, Knowle Hill, where you turn left. Follow Knowle Hill which becomes Newick Lane, initially uphill then swinging sharp right and heading downhill; you swing left, passing an organic farm shop and café, and then take the first left hand road turning, Piccadilly Lane. Look out for a signed footpath a couple of hundred yards along the road, leading off to the right, and then follow this footpath just east of south, firstly through trees then into the meadows, going forward to a footbridge over the Rother. Here, at last, your riverside walking begins. Immediately beyond the river turn left to follow alongside its right bank, but soon the river meanders to the right and you cross it by means of a footbridge to join its left bank and follow it in a straight line, heading just north of east. Although progress looks easy enough on the map, the path isn't always well defined along a field edge, and you need to watch carefully for the point at which the path leaves the field edge to follow close to the bank. Soon you reach another road, Street End Lane, where you are forced away from the river; turn left to follow the lane uphill, the gradient increasing as you continue, but there are ample rewards in the form of fine views back down to the valley.

In a little over half a mile, take the first right-hand road turning, Witherenden Road, and follow it just south of east. This is a lovely ridge-top road in classic Sussex Wealden surroundings and there are good views both left and right, the Rother valley below you to your right. You pass Little Bainden Farm which is to the right then continue on along the road to the next farm, Gillhope Farm, also on the right, where you turn right onto a clearly signed path that goes straight through the farmyard and heads downhill, south-eastwards. Don't pass through the gate into the field immediately below the farm complex, but pass to the left of it and continue south-east, keeping woodland to your right; from here, continue a little further in the same direction, looking out for a stile and path beyond on your right, going into the woods. Go over the stile and follow the path downhill, bending left. The path becomes indistinct on the ground, but aim for the stile at the bottom end of the woods, emerging and following the signed path south-eastwards across the field to arrive back at the Rother. Cross it by means of a footbridge then follow the path as directed through a field beyond. The path is again rather indistinct, the field itself lush and overgrown, but aim for the clearly marked exit; go forward into the next field which is rather less overgrown and aim half-left for a footbridge over a tributary stream. Once over the bridge, bear left, and walk parallel with the stream to arrive back at the Rother. Walk parallel with the Rother, keeping it to your left, for a couple of hundred yards or so, and go forward to and through a gate to arrive at a bridleway; now sadly forced away from the river, you turn left onto the bridleway and head north along it towards Froghole Farm. You're soon signposted onto a rough path running parallel with the main access road into the farmyard, then swing right to pass beside the farm buildings, and swing left up a signed bridleway which you then follow.

The bridleway arrives back on Witherenden Road and you now follow it eastwards, soon passing the fine buildings of Fair Oak Farm which are to your left. Just beyond the farm there's a large house on your right with a prominent partially mock-Tudor front, and immediately before that is a path leading off to the right. You now have a choice. You could follow this path which proceeds in the shade of trees initially, then emerges into open fields and drops steeply, heading south-east, to a bridge over the Rother. If you cross the bridge and bear left, you can in theory walk beside the Rother, free from obstruction (there's one point where you have to walk a little away from the bank to pass from one field to another, but that is all) to the next road crossing, Swife Lane, at Turk's Bridge. However this riverside walk isn't a designated right of way and there's considerable cultivation in some places and long grass in others. You may in fact prefer to stick to Witherenden Road to its junction with Swife Lane, the advantage of this route being the lovely views down to the Rother which you won't get if you remain in the valley. If nevertheless you follow the Rother to Turk's Bridge, you'll need to turn left on to Swife Lane and follow it northwards to arrive back at Witherenden Road.

Head briefly eastwards from the Swife Lane junction along Witherenden Road but almost at once you turn right onto a signed path that passes through the farmyard of Bivelham Farm. The path goes forward, very clearly, to a footbridge over the Rother; cross it, then turn left to follow the right bank of the Rother heading north-eastwards, aiming for a stile at the next field boundary set a little way back from the bank. The first field may well be cultivated, so again take care to avoid any damage to crops. Cross the stile then shortly go over a bridge across another tributary stream, and continue just south of east along what is a public right of way to the next road crossing, the Rother fairly close by to the left. The path over the fields isn't clear on the ground, and there are precious few signposts, but aim for the farm buildings and skirt the left (north-west) side of them and you'll reach the road safely. Turn left to follow the road north-westwards, crossing the Rother shortly then turning right onto the signed footpath very soon after the river crossing. The signpost isn't immediately discernible but it is there, and it's important that you are not tempted onto the bridleway a little further up the road. Having joined the path, follow it north-eastwards along a right hand field edge. Keep along what is a reasonably well-defined path to the corner of the field, then turn hard left and follow the field edge up as far as a stile and footpath sign, which takes you into another field with Bivelham Forge Farm immediately to the left. Continue across the field just south of east, with thick woodland to your left and the Rother coming in from the right; the path is very indistinct, but once you've reached the river bank again, the going gets a lot easier as you can simply follow alongside the Rother on the left bank. You cross a couple of footbridges over tributary streams – the second is a plank bridge preceded by a stile where you need to be very careful! – then go forward to a very clearly-defined path through a crop field. At the end of that field you go over two more bridges in close succession, with the very prominent Witherenden Farm buildings immediately up ahead of you.

Follow the obvious path uphill towards the farm, but about halfway up turn right onto a signed path through a field, and follow it. Keeping the farm buildings close by to your left, aim for the left-hand side of another farm which soon comes into view straight ahead. Exit the field by a clearly signed path, going forward to reach a T-junction with a metalled lane onto which you turn right, following it to reach another T-junction, here meeting the Burwash Common-Stonegate road. Turn left, north-east, onto the road towards Stonegate railway station. The station is only a few hundred yards along the road and if you're breaking your walk at this point there are good services along the London-Tunbridge Wells-Wadhurst-Battle-Hastings line. However if you're progressing on foot towards Etchingham you need to turn right onto a signed bridleway heading eastwards just beyond the main Witherenden Farm road (on the opposite side) but short of the station. The bridleway goes downhill, then ascends an open field and swings to

the right to aim for and cross a bridge over the railway. Beyond the bridge veer slightly left, swinging gently right to pass to the right of the farm buildings of Hammerden. Swing gently from north-east to south-east, picking up a clear path which turns sharply south and heads direct for the railway, but after a hundred yards or so look out for a left (signed) turn; take this turning and descend quite steeply through the woods, then swing to the right and ascend to arrive at the side of the railway. Swing left and walk briefly parallel with the railway then at a signed footpath junction, cross over the railway, taking great care.

Having crossed the railway,

Messing about in boats? This scene is on the East Sussex Rother near Newenden.

you're now looking out over the Rother valley. Keep along the signed path, just west of south, then veer south-eastwards; the course of the path could be impossible to follow when the fields are cultivated, so your best bet is to turn sharp left and follow the field edge round, then, keeping a line of trees ahead of you (east), aim for the right-hand (south) end of the trees. When you reach this point you'll find a signed path junction at which you bear right, briefly southwards, to be reunited with the Rother at the curiously named Wreckery Bridge. Don't cross the bridge but turn left to follow the left (north) bank of the Rother, your exact course probably dependent on crop growth and undergrowth. Keep beside the bank for about half a mile from Wreckery Bridge, enjoying lovely Wealden valley scenery with a number of oast houses in view – a reminder of how close you are to the border with Kent. After this half mile the Rother swings north and you cross it by means of a footbridge; beyond the bridge, swing south-eastwards as signposted to shortly reach another stile. There was at the time of writing a misleading signpost here pointing south-west, but in fact you follow the next field south-eastwards up the hill, aiming for the very obvious Acorn Farm buildings. Join the farm approach road and follow it to reach the Burwash-Ticehurst road; if you wish to detour to the lovely village of Burwash, just a few hundred yards away, turn right here (the River Dudwell section carries a brief description of the village) but to continue your Rother pilgrimage, turn left onto the road.

Walk down the road and soon cross a bridge over the Rother. Follow the road briefly uphill over the level crossing then turn right almost immediately beyond the crossing onto a narrow footpath through the trees, the path descending to arrive at a stile at the bottom end of a field. Bear left into this field, don't follow the right-hand field edge, but walk uphill through the middle of the field, aiming for fingerposts showing a footpath crossroads, and go straight over the crossroads, heading just east of north. The way is clear initially, but soon the ground falls away steeply; pause here and enjoy the view, just west of north, to the outstandingly attractive assembly of buildings that make up Old Shoyswell Manor Farm, in a magnificent setting. To proceed from your fine vantage point, descend quite steeply towards these buildings, aiming for a gate and stile at the foot of the hill. The path is very ill-defined, but with this gate and stile as your immediate goal, there is no difficulty. Go through the gate (or over the stile) and almost immediately bear right through another gate/stile to join a wider bridlepath, following this uphill to a junction of paths. Turn right here onto a firm track which then swings left, just east of north (avoiding the tempting looking path heading away south-eastwards here), and follow the track uphill to arrive at a T-junction with the metalled Sheepstreet Lane. Turn right to follow the lane. The road walk is pleasant with lovely views to the Limden valley to your left and very impressive residential properties to admire by the roadside.

After about half a mile of road walking, look out for a post box on the left, just beyond which you turn right onto a footpath signed by a stone plinth. The path, which you follow initially just west of south, is beautifully defined, and well signed; it swings just east of south, and enters a wooded area, narrowing somewhat and now descending quite steeply. A surprise then awaits you, for suddenly you emerge into an open area of rough green valley-floor pasture which contrasts vividly with the ridge-top and woodland walking that has characterised the last couple of miles. Keep to the extreme right edge of the open pasture, with thick vegetation to your right, in due course arriving at a subsidiary channel of the Rother. You're forced to swing left (eastwards) and walk very briefly beside this channel, but look out very carefully in just a few yards for a narrow path leading off to the right. Join this path which goes over two footbridges, the first one over the tributary channel and the second, almost immediately afterwards, over the Rother. The railway is just ahead of you; don't go forward to cross the line but rather swing left and walk eastwards along the south (right) bank of the Rother. The walk appears not to be a designated right of way and the going is often rough with only spasmodic and irregular stretches of riverside path, but there are no difficulties, and a gate provides access to a road, Church Hill. Turn right onto it and follow it over the railway, very soon arriving at the main street of Etchingham. The somewhat unusual name of the village, which in 1610 was known as Itchingham, is derived from its being on the site of a "hamm" or watermeadow owned by a tribe known as the Eccingas. The village boasts a massive 14th century church which was the baronial church of Sir William de Echyngham; a fine memorial to him in chainmail lies in front of the altar, while other features of interest in the church include choir stalls with misericords and

The East Sussex Rother near Wittersham complete with swans, sheep and lots of electricity.

15th century brasses. In the Middle Ages there was a fortified manor of the de Echyngham family which stood roughly where the station is now, and which guarded a crossing point of the Rother that was navigable upstream to this point for the ships of that time.

Limden detour

At Etchingham you might choose to detour along the Limden, a tributary of the Rother, perhaps following it upstream then taking the train from Stonegate back to Etchingham, although frustratingly little riverside walking is possible. To access it, cross the level crossing and head briefly eastwards onto the A265, soon crossing the bridge over the Rother. Immediately beyond there are steps leading down to the left; take these steps, straightaway noting the confluence of the Rother with the Limden, then follow the right bank of the Limden upstream away from Etchingham. Soon a footbridge switches you to the left bank and shortly after that the river meanders a little way to the right, but there's still a pleasant valley/riverside feel to the walk. You cross a footbridge over a subsidiary stream and then proceed over the field, keeping the Limden to your right, heading just east of north to Fysie Lane. Cross Fysie Lane and continue along a grassy path with the Limden to your right, enjoying what is most attractive valley scenery. You pass a footbridge* with options of a path straight on or over the footbridge and here is your first difficulty; the former path should go forward to another footbridge over the Limden, but at the time of writing it had disintegrated and the land beyond it was an impassable morass. If the council have restored the footbridge and path when you read this, continue in a straight line just west of north through the marsh beyond the bridge, ascending slightly to the top of the field to meet a bridleway coming from the north**. Turn left onto this bridleway, crossing into the next field then veering immediately left and proceeding gently south-westwards downhill to a footbridge over the Limden which you cross and continue along the obvious bridlepath back to the road. If the collapsed footbridge hasn't been restored and/or the land beyond is still impassable you have a choice. You could either retrace your steps to the road and turn right, following the road to where the bridlepath meets it. For a longer walk, you could cross the footbridge marked * above and then take the obvious path heading north-east, soon becoming a clear farm track. Continue all the way along the farm track – a good mile – to reach the B2099; turn left and follow this road for about half a mile, turning next left down the lane to Swiftsden Farm. Follow the lane to the next farm, bearing slightly right to pass the farm buildings, then veer left, just east of south, onto a straight grassy path bringing you to the point marked ** above, with a good view to the Limden valley. Turn sharp right to continue via the bridleway to the road.

You are now faced with a lengthy but unavoidable road walk of around 2 miles. The lanes to Kitchingham Farm and Burgham, leading away to the right, offer bridge crossings of the Limden but it's impossible for you to access the bank in either case. The views to the Limden valley are good from the road, and although you can't see the river, the walking is reasonably enjoyable. Finally, after 2 miles or so, you reach a road junction with Ticehurst signposted to your right; take this road, soon crossing a bridge over the Limden and then rising, admiring a very fine house and garden on the right just beyond the bridge. More or less opposite the house to the left is a plinth indicating a public footpath and you take this towards Wedd's Farm. However before taking this path, actually a metalled lane, I strongly recommend you detour up the road into Ticehurst, just half a mile away. Ticehurst is a lovely village with many old weatherboarded and tile-hung cottages and several traditional shops including at the time of writing a butcher, greengrocer and bookshop combined with a coffee shop. The church of St Mary dates back to the 13th and 14th centuries and contains wooden choir stalls carved by Robert Thompson whose trademark was the addition of lifelike church mice to his carvings; his work, with this distinctive feature, can be seen in hundreds of churches including York Minster and Westminster Abbey. Returning to the Wedd's Farm lane, you follow the lane to the farm, keeping the Limden a little way away to your left. When you reach the farm buildings, you're clearly signposted round the right-hand side of them, then you veer left to pass the left-hand edge of a pond just beyond the farm buildings. Just beyond the pond you reach a gate on your right leading into a field; go through the gate and follow a clear path westwards through the field, a footpath signpost reassuring you as you continue, and with the Limden a short distance away down to your left. You skirt the right side of one patch of wood and approach another, your path veering left here and then shortly right to proceed westwards to a bridge crossing over the Limden and then a gate leading you to the buildings of Lymden Farm. Proceed through the farmyard to arrive at Lymden Lane. Just to the right is the lane's bridge crossing of the river, and this will be the last you see of the river, for its source is hidden in the trees a short way beyond the road. Your Limden exploration thus ends here. Turn left to walk up Lymden Lane, climbing steeply to reach the village of Stonegate; to get to the station, cross over at the crossroads on to Ticehurst Road and follow it past the village church and then on downhill for a little over a mile, the station clearly signposted on the left. There is a regular train service back to Etchingham, just a few minutes away by rail.

It isn't possible to follow the Rother immediately south-east of Etchingham, and indeed between Etchingham and Salehurst there is unfortunately very little of the Rother to see, and no opportunity for riverside walking as such. In fact it is hard to ascertain from the OS mapping which of the various stretches of water in the valley between these two villages is actually the Rother! Whichever stretch of water does in fact qualify for that title, you can at least be reassured that you are and will remain in the Rother valley. Starting from the church in Etchingham's village centre, follow the main road eastwards to just short of the level crossing, but immediately before the crossing (the Rother is on the other side of the railway) turn right onto the metalled road signposted Lundsford Farm. Follow it over the river Dudwell and go forward to the gate on the left almost immediately opposite a gate on the right, and before the first house. Pass through the left gate onto a faint path that runs roughly parallel with the railway, then descend across the meadow, aiming for a gate at the bottom, keeping Lundsford Farm just to your right. At the bottom by the gate, there's a footpath junction; you need to take the path heading south-east, keeping the railway just to your left. Initially you have to keep your distance from the railway because of the surrounding vegetation, but soon the path returns to follow not only parallel with but immediately below the railway embankment.

Keep along the path but in a few hundred yards turn left onto a signed path and cross the railway.

Once over the railway, bear immediately right to continue south-east through the meadow. Initially the path keeps the railway embankment just to the right, but then veers away from it to the left; aim initially for a stile and then join a clear path that follows the left-hand edge of the meadow, with thick vegetation and the ground rising to your left. Pass to the left of an attractive lake and now swing just east of south, your obvious path proceeding down to the disused mill at Northbridge. To your left is a somewhat stagnant strip of water, but shortly to your right you are reunited with the Rother, and you stick to its left bank as you reach the mill buildings, swinging eastwards to arrive at the Northbridge-Robertsbridge road. Your route turns left here towards the roundabout with the busy A21, but by turning right you can walk on into Robertsbridge. The village, which has a useful railway station, takes its name from Robert de St Martin, a nobleman of Norman descent who founded a Cistercian abbey by the eastern Rother (see below) towards the end of the 12th century; the "bridge" of Robertsbridge is actually the bridge over the Rother that you will have seen on reaching the Northbridge-Robertsbridge road, the bridge dating back to the founding of the abbey. Robertsbridge boasts a number of timber-framed houses but has no buildings of real note, although Pevsner describes the Congregational Methodist Church as "truly horrible!"

Returning to the route, proceed to the roundabout with the A21, crossing straight over and enjoying a pleasant walk along the minor road to Salehurst, less than a mile away; the Rother is situated a short distance to your right, going roughly parallel with the road. Salehurst's most prominent feature is the large gaunt church used by Robertsbridge, which dates back to the 13th century. It has a quite magnificent 14th century tower, visible for miles, and also boasts a particularly remarkable font, carved with salamanders running round the foot; tradition has it that it was given to the church by Richard the Lionheart in gratitude for being released from imprisonment in Bavaria by Abbot William of Robertsbridge. Another attractive feature of the village is a pub right on the route, called Salehurst Halt after the railway halt of the same name that stood close by. Just beyond the pub the road bends sharp left, but you keep straight ahead along a bridlepath that soon bends south-eastwards and descends, crossing the course of the old Robertsbridge to Tenterden railway line, much of which has been preserved as the Kent & East Sussex Railway. You will see more of this railway as you continue. Now you go forward along the track to arrive at Church Bridge, a crossing of the Rother; at last the Rother is clear and discernible, and after the disappointing miles from Etchingham with so little riverside walking, the river will from now on never be far away and indeed for much of your walk from here you will remain within shouting distance of it.

Having crossed the bridge you continue southwards to a T-junction with the Abbey approach road. Follow this road eastwards, enjoying lovely views back to the tower of Salehurst Church; the road bends sharply right and then left, passing the house into which the remains of Robertsbridge Abbey, which was founded in 1176, is incorporated.

Continue on along the road, then just as it bends right again you join a path leaving the road and heading along an obvious path in a generally easterly direction, with the Rother across the meadows to your left. In roughly a quarter of a mile there's a clear footpath signpost, with one arm of the signpost showing a path heading southwards towards the woods. Immediately before this signpost, look carefully for some steps leaving the path (the one you have been following) to your left. Walk up these steps and go forward along a very narrow path, keeping the Rother now immediately to your left and a ditch to your right. The path is not only narrow but overgrown and potentially very slippery in places. After a few hundred yards the Rother bends to the left, passing an old air raid shelter, and goes under a bridge carrying the old railway. The very narrow path widens here to provide easier walking beside the river under the bridge, and beyond the bridge you enter a broad meadow; although this isn't a designated right of way on maps, there is no difficulty of access and you are able to follow beside the Rother through the meadow, shortly (just over a quarter of a mile from the old railway crossing) arriving at the B2244. Turn left onto the road, cross the river by the bridge, then turn immediately right onto the riverside footpath which, keeping the Rother to the right, proceeds pleasantly to Bodiam Bridge about a mile beyond the B2244. You emerge onto the road at Bodiam Bridge, keeping the castle directly ahead, and although your route now bears right and proceeds across the bridge to join the right bank, you may wish to detour to visit the castle, described with some justification as a "storybook castle." Following a raid on Rye by the French in 1377, it was feared that the French might sail a further flotilla further inland via the Rother, and Bodiam Castle was built as a result. In fact the castle was not to see any action until the English Civil War and was then dismantled; it was subsequently rescued and restored, and it was acquired in due course by the National Trust. Its most impressive features are its gatehouse (with portcullis), Great Hall, servants' hall, chapel and kitchen, and there is also an excellent café(it's not necessary to pay to enter the castle in order to patronise it) and lovely grounds.

Back on the route, having crossed the bridge you then bear immediately left onto a signed path along the embankment, the Rother now to your left. However you could make a further detour up to Bodiam station on the Kent & East Sussex Railway, a line which linked Robertsbridge with Headcorn in Kent. The section of line between Robertsbridge and Tenterden, incorporating Bodiam, was opened in 1900 and closed to passengers in 1954, but the line between Tenterden and Bodiam has now been reopened as a preserved railway. Back on the embankment on the east side of Bodiam Bridge, the path is soon signposted to the right, away from the river, but you're able to continue along the riverbank all the way to Newenden Bridge; it isn't a designated right of way but access is no problem, and although there are a few gates they're not locked and may be left open. You could decide to follow the embankment, but it is tougher going, and you may prefer to stick to the actual river bank along much of which there is a clear track. It is lovely walking, the Rother with you all the way and beautiful meadows all around, and on the first half of the three miles or so from Bodiam to

Newenden you'll enjoy gorgeous views back to Bodiam Castle. This is extremely popular fishing country, and you may see a number of fishermen as you walk.

At length, you arrive at Newenden Bridge which carries the busy A28 over the Rother. A mile to your right is Northiam with ample amenities, and although your route bears left to cross the river, you may wish to detour to visit Northiam before continuing. The showpiece of Northiam is an ancient battered oak on the village green, held together by chains, and all round the green are fine examples of weatherboarded 18th century houses, while the church has a tall stone spire hidden behind a Norman base. Queen Elizabeth I dined at Northiam in 1573 whilst journeying through Kent and Sussex, and she left some shoes here which are kept at a large 17th century timber-framed house named Brickwall. The finest attraction in Northiam is Great Dixter, a 15th century house with magnificent gardens which were designed by Edwin Lutyens and which are arguably the finest in Sussex. Back on the route, you cross the river at Newenden Bridge as stated above, entering Kent in which you will stay for the next few miles. Before continuing beside the Rother you may wish to enjoy a drink or meal at the White Hart pub just beyond the river, and perhaps detour to the village of Newenden which is just a short way to the north along the main road; Newenden, where the first Carmelites to arrive in England are said to have settled, is a trim little village, its church a fragment of a much larger medieval building with a fine Norman font, carved with the design of a dragon and other fabulous beasts.

A fine view of the East Sussex Rother taken from the Ypres Tower of St Mary's Church in Rye.

Where have all the tourists gone? A quiet and beautiful corner of Rye, just below which the East Sussex Rother, the Brede and the Tillingham all converge.

Beyond Newenden Bridge, you need to look out for and join a signed footpath just north of the bridge on the right. Follow the footpath round the back of the cricket field, going forward to and passing through a gate to join a riverside public footpath; a lovely walk follows, the Rother to your right, initially passing a small fleet of pleasure boats, and although there is initially housing to your left you leave that behind and the surroundings once more become completely unspoilt. You swing south-eastwards with the river to cross the preserved railway, then return to the riverside, ignoring a tempting path going straight ahead from the crossing gate. Beyond the crossing, the river bends left and shortly beyond the bend you approach a large house marked on maps as New Barn; the way ahead is blocked and you need to drop down off the bank, going forward to reach a path going left to right. Turn right and follow this path through a gate, then proceed for a few yards until you reach a path going off to the left, keeping to the left side of a channel on an embankment. Bear left along this clear path which soon swings south of east, separated by the channel from the Rother embankment; soon you reach a fork, the left path providing the shorter route but in fact both paths, hemmed in by channels to the right and left, head inexorably for the pumping station and footbridge crossing of Maytham Sewer at Maytham Wharf. Cross the footbridge and bear slightly right along the obvious path, heading for a row of houses, then swing left along the clear track, keeping the houses to the right. Go forward to a T-junction with a minor road, turn right onto the road and follow it, initially eastwards, soon bending a little north of east and arriving at a crossing of Potman's Heath Channel at the hamlet of Potman's Heath.

Cross the channel then immediately bear right onto a path along the channel's east bank, heading south-eastwards; soon the Rother comes in from the right, Potman's Heath Channel merging with it, and you won't lose sight of the Rother again for virtually the whole of the rest of your journey. You have a choice between a path which can be rather rough, immediately adjacent to the water, or an embankment to the left of the path, but often there's fencing which blocks progress along the embankment. You pass a pumping station and cross the Wittersham-Peasmarsh road at Blackwall Bridge, noting Wittersham Church standing proudly on a hill to the left. Wittersham is regarded as the "capital" of the Isle of Oxney, which in turn has something of a "cut off" island feel, still surrounded by water, although only ditches and streams remain of the wide waters that once covered the Rother levels. The massive battlemented tower of the chiefly 14th century church at Wittersham, such a conspicuous feature for Rother-side walkers, was added at the end of the 15th century. Now on the Sussex Border Path, plough on along the riverside path, choosing between that and the embankment. The grass can be rough and the surface isn't always even, but it is still very pleasant walking indeed with so much to enjoy; swans and wading birds gracing the surface of the river, boats and canoes carefully navigating their way up or down stream, a plethora of anglers hoping for a good "catch," lovely views across the meadows and rolling hills of Kent (to your left) and East Sussex (to your right), and constantly colourful vegetation all around you. OS maps suggest the official path and Sussex Border Path leave the riverside temporarily, but in fact there's no difficulty in keeping to the riverside throughout. Passing now back into East Sussex, you cross the Wittersham-Playden road at New Bridge, then continue, now slipping more decisively south-eastwards. To your right across the river is the particularly fine set of hilltop buildings of Thornsdale Farm, with a splendid oast house, while ahead of you to the left is Stone Cliff, a prominent hillside just to the south of the historic village of Stone-in-Oxney. This was once an island village, standing on the Isle of Oxney before the marshes were drained, and the Ferry Inn still displays a road toll sign. In the tower of the restored 15th century church are a Roman Mithras-cult altar stone and the fossilised remains of an iguanodon dinosaur.

In due course, with the next road bridge crossing in sight, you find your way ahead beside the river barred but a clearly marked path takes you just the few yards to the Appledore-Rye road. Turn right onto it and then immediately left, arriving at the disused Iden lock, the gates of which were constructed at the start of the 19th century. You use the bridge at the lock to cross straight over the Royal Military Canal which comes in from your left, and looking to the right you'll see the Canal linking up with the Rother; the canal, built in 1807 as a response to the threat of invasion during the Napoleonic Wars, was just 30ft wide at its broadest point, but was capable of carrying both troops and equipment between Kent and Sussex. Having crossed the canal, turn immediately right to follow the obvious path southwards then just west of south, keeping the combined canal/Rother to your right, and now sharing your route with the Sussex Border Path, Saxon Shore Way and Royal Military Canal Way!! The Sussex Border Path runs for 135 miles between Emsworth and Rye, aiming to follow as closely as possible the border between Sussex and its neighbouring counties of Hampshire, Surrey and Kent, although it rarely if ever follows the actual border and makes frequent incursions into the neighbouring counties. The Saxon Shore Way, meanwhile, takes the walker for some 160 miles round sections of the coastline of Kent and Sussex, from Gravesend to Hastings, following the coastline as it was around 1500 years ago before the North Kent marshes and Romney Marsh existed. It takes its name from a line of fortifications built along the coastline as it was in the 3rd century AD, and the invaders, known as Saxons, who came from the southern region of what is now Denmark.

The going is now very straightforward all the way to the A259 crossing at Rye; the views ahead to the hilltop town of Rye are very good indeed, as are the views immediately across the river to the wooded hillsides around the villages of Iden and Playden. You pass another old lock and cross the Union Channel which comes in from the left, noting how much wider the Rother has become just since it joined with the Canal, and how much more estuarine it is now in appearance. You pass under quite a low railway bridge, and very shortly arrive at the A259 crossing where all but the most stalwart, single-minded or rushed walkers will leave the riverside and turn right to cross the river and enter the beautiful town of Rye. During the Middle Ages this hilltop town, once a hill fort, was almost ringed by waters, standing as it did on a promontory linked to the mainland by a neck of land in turn guarded by the estuaries of the rivers Rother and Tillingham. It was once an important port, exporting wool and iron, and became one of the Cinque Ports in the middle of the 14th century, but as a result of silting from the 16th century it was left 2 miles inland. It is now primarily a tourist attraction, its cobbled narrow streets crammed with beautifully preserved historic houses, many weatherboarded, tile-hung or timber-framed. Among its finest buildings are the church of St Mary, with its remarkable clock containing what is possibly the oldest functioning pendulum in England; the 14th century Landgate, the last remaining of Rye's three fortified gates; the 13th century Ypres Tower, formerly a prison and now a museum; the fine part-13th century Mermaid Inn in the sloping cobbled Mermaid Street; the 17th century Old Grammar School in the High Street; the 15th century timber-framed Flushing Inn and the 18th century Town Hall in Market Street; the three-storeyed 15th century Fletcher's House in Lion Street; and, in West Street, the 18th century Lamb House where Henry James lived and E.F. Benson wrote the famous *Mapp & Lucia* books which were all set in Rye.

Returning to the A259 crossing of the river, go over the Rother by this road and then immediately turn right. Ahead is a metalled cycle track which is the course of another old railway, the Rye-Camber line known as the Camber Tramway; it opened in July

1895, but was requisitioned by the Navy at the start of the Second World War, and never reopened. Don't follow the cycle track, but almost at once bear right to pass through the gate and join a lovely grassy embankment path on the left bank of the Rother. In due course you pass to the right of a lake, beyond which the path swings left to arrive at a metalled track, and on reaching it you turn right onto it and follow it, keeping Rye golf course to your left. You arrive at a gate and a sign saying "Footpath to Camber;" pass through the gate and continue along the path, keeping a fence to the left. Very shortly you join a right fork which takes you away from the fence and forward to the riverbank again, then having joined the bank continue along it to Camber Sands. It's an exciting moment to reach the point at which the Rother flows into the sea. Across the river to the west you can see the houses of the village of Rye Harbour and its nature reserve that extends westwards to Winchelsea Beach, with the cliffs around Fairlight providing an impressive backcloth; to the left, Camber and Broomhill Sands, a paradise for holidaymakers and beachlovers, stretch out seemingly for ever. It is a very fine climax to your walk along the Rother. You may choose to return to Rye the same way, or, if you feel that is too much walking, the village of Camber is a short distance away across the sands to your left, with not only a reasonable range of amenities but an excellent bus link with Rye.

THE RIVER TILLINGHAM

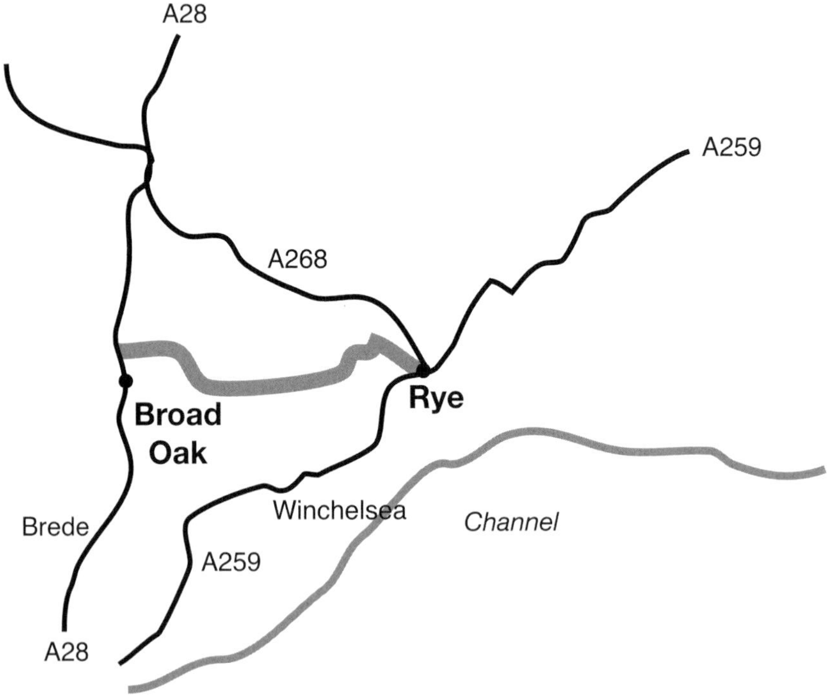

A28

A259

A268

Broad
Oak

Rye

Brede

Winchelsea

Channel

A259

A28

THE RIVER TILLINGHAM

Length:	7 miles.
Start:	Broad Oak.
Finish:	Rye.
Public transport:	Regular buses between Hastings and Tenterden via Broad Oak(not Sundays); regular buses linking Rye with Hastings, Folkestone and Dover; regular trains serving Rye on the Brighton-Eastbourne-Hastings line.
Refreshments:	Pub and shop at Broad Oak; pubs, cafes, shops at Rye. No refreshments on the route itself.
Conditions:	A very easy and delightful walk albeit not all on designated rights of way. Physically access presents no difficulty but it may be prudent to seek permission to walk sections that are not along designated rights of way or permissive paths.

Following the river: Starting from the centre of Broad Oak village, follow the A28 northwards towards Northiam, dropping quite steeply to reach the river crossing at Arnold Bridge about half a mile to the north of Broad Oak. Cross the bridge and immediately bear right onto a driveway which is a public right of way, keeping the river, very narrow at this point, to the right. As the driveway veers away to the left, join a signed path which crosses over the river and keeps it to the left, with Wagmary Wood immediately to the right. The river remains narrow but exuberant with numerous twists and turns and the occasional little waterfall. Shortly you're signposted back onto the other side and you now keep the river to your right, soon entering Furnace Wood with your path passing through the trees and then emerging to follow a field edge, with fencing to your left and the river immediately to your right. You arrive at a road crossing, Furnace Lane, with Furnace Farm immediately opposite; turn right to cross the river then immediately bear left along a signed track which keeps the farm buildings to the left, while within view to your right is a particularly fine oast house. Just beyond the buildings the path divides, and here you take the left fork, soon arriving back beside the river. You can now enjoy a lovely walk beside the river through delightful meadow scenery, keeping the river to your left, and going forward to arrive a junction with the metalled Hundredhouse Lane.

Beyond Hundredhouse Lane there is no designated right of way beside the river but in

The river Brede and the river Tillingham can both be seen in this view from Rye towards Winchelsea, again taken from the Ypres Tower atop St Mary's Church.

fact there's no problem with access. Turn left to cross Hundredhouse Bridge and follow the lane briefly, but go through the gate giving access to the first field on the right beyond the bridge, and walk down to the bank. Veer left (north) shortly to pass through another gate, but beyond that there's no difficulty in keeping to the left bank of the river. You pass a footbridge and junction with right of way just to the north of Newman's Farm, then keep going beside the river for just under half a mile to reach another footbridge; cross this bridge then turn left to follow a permissive path along the right bank of the river which is now a little wider than at the start but is a straighter narrower channel and at this point resembles a miniature canal. After just under half a mile, you pass another footbridge, where the permissive path ends, but keep going on the same side, with the river to your left. This isn't a designated right of way, and indeed it is necessary to cross a wooden fence at one point; it is low enough for it not to be an obstruction as such, but if you are uncomfortable about proceeding, seek permission from the relevant landowner. Heading just a little south of east, you proceed forward to another footbridge, marked on maps as Tillingham Bridge. Use the footbridge to cross over the river, then bear right through the next gate to resume your riverside walk, now keeping the noticeably widening river to your right; this is all delightful scenery, with hills and woodlands to be seen on either side of the valley, and quite soon now you will see the buildings of Rye, dominated by its hilltop church, just ahead.

Progress remains straightforward, albeit this is not a designated right of way; there are gates, but you will find them either left open or able to be opened. When I walked it, there was just one gate that was locked, but I was able to cross an adjacent low fence built over a raised concrete slab. If in doubt, again seek permission from the landowner. Looking north-eastwards, you'll see the splendid hilltop redbrick Leasam House Farm; as you get closer to this, you'll find yourself forced a little away from the river onto an embankment that leads through a scattering of trees, and you then need to veer a little right to cross a wooden bridge that is constructed a little like a cattle grid, and may require some care to negotiate. You then return to the riverside and very shortly you will meet a signpost indicating you are now on a designated right of way which has come in from the left. This is the High Weald Landscape Trail, which runs for 90 miles from Horsham to Rye via East Grinstead. Following this trail for the time being, you keep to the riverside initially but are then forced away from it by wire fencing, being obliged to walk up to a gate; having crossed it you can then return to the left bank of the river and follow it, an area of suburban housing visible immediately over the other side. Keeping the river to your right, you now go forward to pass the magnificent redbrick Rolvendene Farm. Beyond the farm there's a choice of paths, but you stick to the riverside one, observing how wide the river is now and how impressive it is compared with the tiny channel at Broad Oak only 6 miles back. The grassy path now becomes a concrete one, with allotment gardens to the left, but in a couple of hundred yards you join a path forking off to the right, which keeps you immediately beside the river(still to your right) and takes you to a junction with Udimore Road. Cross straight over this road, and

The greensward beside the river Tillingham at Rye, a very popular spot on fine days but virtually deserted on this freezing March afternoon.

The river Tillingham is the smallest of the three "name" rivers which meet at Rye, but here, close to its "T-junction" meeting with the Brede, it still looks impressive.

continue along a footpath which soon goes forward to cross the railway. Beyond the crossing, go forward to emerge at the A259 Winchelsea Road which you also cross, keeping the river to your right. Separating you from the river, now sufficiently wide to allow boats to be moored on it, is a greensward which is immensely popular with visitors in fine weather, while immediately to your left is Rye's lovely centre. Follow the greensward to its very end then bear right onto a lane which leads you past a café and continues for a few yards, the Tillingham to your right but now out of sight. As the lane swings to the left, walk up the slope and, looking to your right, you'll see the meeting of the River Tillingham with the River Brede. It is a true T-junction of rivers! Your Tillingham walk is at an end, and it merely remains for you to retrace your steps down the lane to the greensward, cross over the main road and use one of the many streets leading off it to access Rye's delights, described more fully in the section devoted to the East Sussex Rother.

A delightful stretch of the river Tillingham, in attractive countryside between
Broad Oak and Rye.

THE RIVER UCK

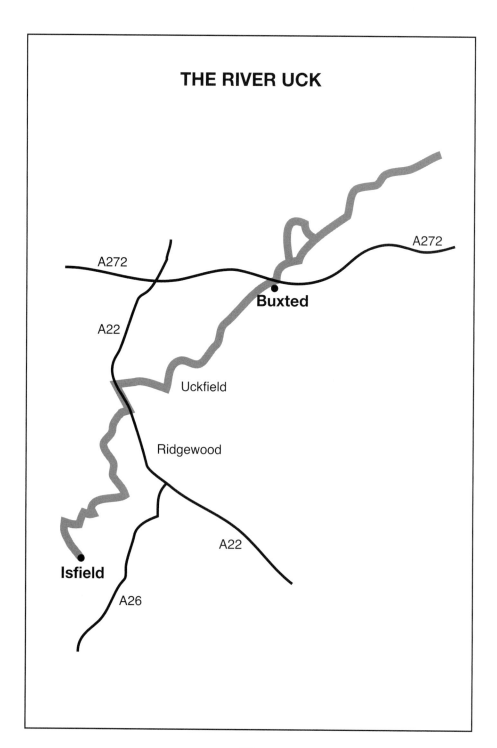

THE RIVER UCK

Length:	Approximately 12 miles.
Start:	Isfield.
Finish:	Buxted.
Public transport:	Regular buses to and from Lewes and Tunbridge Wells, serving Isfield and Uckfield; regular trains between Buxted and Uckfield.
Refreshments:	Occasional café and pub at Isfield; shops, pubs and cafes at Uckfield; pub and shop at Buxted.
Conditions:	This isn't the most rewarding riverside walk in Sussex, but there are a number of items of interest en route and the scenery is pleasant throughout.

Your walk starts at the old Lavender Line station at Isfield (see the river Ouse chapter above) immediately adjacent to where buses stop on the Lewes-Tunbridge Wells route. Turning right out of the old station complex, walk through the village centre, and in about three quarters of a mile you reach the bridge crossing of the Uck, but just before the bridge, turn right to follow the river bank along a signed path. Soon you reach a house – the footpath actually encroaches on to the driveway! – and it's important to follow the footpath signposts, aiming for farm buildings straight ahead of you, following a clear track which takes you into the farmyard. Bear left as shown by the signpost, and ignoring the footpath arrow pointing away to the right, go straight on ahead across the meadow to be reunited with the river bank. Now enjoy a delightful walk along the right bank of the river, passing a weir, with extensive meadows all around you; you arrive at a metal kissing gate, which you pass through, then almost immediately bear left across a footbridge to begin a walk along the left bank of the river. This is quite beautiful walking in unspoilt countryside, with its mixture of woodland and meadows. Your bankside walk passes under the old Lewes-Uckfield railway, and continues on past two meanders and over a footbridge where the Uck splits into two channels. Beyond the bridge go on ahead across a field to reach a narrow road. Turn left onto the road, passing a river indicator beyond which you turn immediately left on to a lovely green path (not a designated right of way but with no difficulty of access) which proceeds very pleasantly past woodland which lies to the left. Soon you find yourself back on the right bank of the Uck. Follow the bank until you are forced to bear right through some thick undergrowth to reach a field, then bear left to follow the left-hand field edge. You soon pass another splendid weir and very shortly beyond it you veer left to ascend gently onto the course of the old railway line which you follow north-eastwards towards Uckfield. It isn't a designated right of way but access is no problem; there are good views from the embankment down to the Uck, and it is most enjoyable walking.

In about half a mile, you reach a gate to your right, with the buildings of Owlsbury Farm immediately beyond. Bear right here then immediately left onto a footpath running diagonally uphill, aiming for a gate. Go through the gate, bear right and walk past the farm buildings, keeping them to your right. Beyond the buildings you veer left to follow

an obvious path through open fields down to the A22. Turn right at the bottom, just before the road embankment, and follow the field edge parallel with the road, soon reaching a stile to your left. Cross it and follow a badly overgrown path to the A22, then cross the road and turn left to follow it north-westwards; in due course you cross over the Uck and continue the short distance to the B2102. Turn right to follow this road – the Uck running parallel to the right, through an industrial estate – and arrive at a T-junction with Uckfield High Street, here turning left to follow the High Street into the town centre. Uckfield isn't the prettiest town in Sussex, but it does have some features of interest, notably the 3-storeyed Maiden's Head, a large bow-windowed Georgian pub; the 5-bayed grey-brick Church House in Church Street; the Old

Many "name" rivers in Sussex are no wider or more impressive-looking than a host of un-named ones. This is the modest flow of the Uck near Buxted.

Grammar School with its timber-framed early 17th century wing; and Hooke Hall, boasting fine early 18th century chequer brick. In October 2000 the Uck flooded spectacularly and caused devastation to many of the town's shops, homes and businesses. If you arrive here on a dry hot summer's day you might find it hard to believe it happened.

Turn right off the High Street into Hempstead Road, going forward into Hempstead Lane; this becomes a footpath that arrives at a T-junction with Brown's Lane, and here you turn left then first right into a continuation of Hempstead Lane. Descend to the river, passing Hempstead Mill – there is a charming waterfall here – then turn right along a signed path which follows immediately alongside the Uck before the river goes away to the right. You cross a footbridge, keeping a tributary channel to your right, now briefly on the Wealdway (see the chapter devoted to the Cuckmere), and heading north-eastwards. Soon you reach another footbridge; here the Wealdway goes off to the left, but you continue north-eastwards and proceed through the delightful surroundings of Buxted Park. The original house at Buxted Park was pulled down in the early 18th century, and the present house was completed in 1725. In 1931 it was bought by Basil Ionides, the architect, who altered it considerably and made it what has been described as a "magpies' nest" of bits from other houses that were being demolished or had been blitzed in the Second World War; in due course it was to become a luxury hotel. You soon pass a lake, just beyond which a signed path goes off to the right and brings you back to the Uck, and it would be possible to follow the left bank for a very short while by way of a narrow but reasonably clear path. However there is no designated right of way and in order to progress you need to make your way back cross-country, as it were, to the main path, which goes forward to reach the busy A272.

Cross the A272 and follow it eastwards over the river, climbing and soon passing Buxted railway station which is to your left, then shortly beyond the station, turn left into Church Road. You pass Buxted village church, which boasts a 13th century west tower, a Jacobean pulpit and 13th century chest, and a magnificent moulded plaster ceiling in the chancel with an image of St Margaret, an 11th century Queen of Scotland, embossed onto it. Keep on along Church Road, passing the right turn to Park View, then as the road bends to the right, look out for a signed footpath going off to the left, and take this path. It starts as a proper path but soon enters a field and you proceed across the middle of the field towards the railway; close to the far end of the field, look to your left for a bridge crossing of the railway, bear left to cross the line using the bridge then, continuing in the same direction, drop down steeply through open pasture to the river, aiming for a footbridge. Don't cross the bridge but bear right just before it and go forward to a gate, passing through it and continuing through the meadow, keeping the Uck to your left. This is not a designated right of way but there was at the time of writing no difficulty of access, there appeared to be a clear path, and judging by the footprints, it was and is well used. You approach the end of the meadow, with trees immediately ahead of you; although there's a crude ledge immediately above the river, it is unsafe for you to attempt to walk it, and you need to look out for an obvious path going off right into the woods shortly before the meadow ends. Follow this path and continue through the woods, now walking parallel with a railway embankment to your right. This has the appearance of a pretty rustic railway that fell victim to the Beeching axe of the 1960's, but in fact it's still a functioning part of the Southern railway network, linking Uckfield and Buxted with Crowborough, Eridge and Oxted. Soon you see a bridge to your right, and as you arrive at the bridge you reach a T-junction of paths; turn right and follow the footpath under the railway, now temporarily on the Vanguard Way, a 66-mile walk linking East Croydon with Newhaven. Continue beyond the bridge briefly through the woods, soon emerging into open pasture at the foot of quite a steep escarpment. Do not proceed straight up the central slope, but aim half-left and then proceed up the left, gentler side of the escarpment, keeping woodland and a murky pool fairly close to your left. Walk on up the hill, going forward to a rather rickety wooden stile at the edge of woodland, then cross the stile – carefully! – and immediately arrive at a **crossroads of footpaths.****** Turn left here, leaving the Vanguard Way, and follow the path downhill then uphill through the woods, the ground quite juicy underfoot as you climb. You emerge into Buxted Wood Lane – the transition from path to lane is very obvious – and, almost immediately you do so, look out for a footpath going off to the left, and follow it. This proceeds north-eastwards in a reasonably straight line, firstly through woodland, then through the bottom of a private garden, then fields interspersed by an area of woodland; the path is impressively well signposted, you cannot go wrong, and emerging from the woods, you can now enjoy superb views to your left, down to the Uck valley and beyond. You reach a large white house and swing hard right, rising very slightly to reach Howbourne Lane, then bear left along this lane, walking downhill to the valley bottom.

Continue along the lane past Howbourne Farm and you'll arrive at a gate marked Grey's Wood Farm. Immediately to the left of that is a stile; go over the stile but instead of going straight ahead, turn hard left and descend briefly to arrive at the south bank of the Uck. You can now follow the south bank all the way to the next road crossing just south of Hastingford Farm, with only one brief detour needed to get round a field boundary hedge. It is lovely peaceful walking and although it is not designated as a right of way, access presented no problem at the time of researching this section. As you approach the road crossing, aim for the gate and stile just to the right; cross over the stile onto the road then turn left to cross the little river bridge, and look out for a charming waterfall on the west side of the bridge. Immediately beyond the bridge, turn right onto a signed path, and now continue alongside the north bank of the Uck all the way to Huggett's Furnace. Initially you may find it easier to walk beside the parallel driveway, but it is worth the little extra effort to walk by the infant river, which is a delightful spectacle and prone to be active even during or after a dry spell. At length the driveway goes off to the left, but you continue along the bank, negotiating a number of stiles en route, arriving at a T-junction with a track. Huggett's Furnace, a superb collection of old buildings, is to the left, but you turn right to arrive at a charming mill from which the waters of the Uck emerge. This is as close to its source as you can go. There is no easily available public transport anywhere near this point, so retrace your steps all the way back to the **crossroads of footpaths** that is quadruple asterisked above. Go straight over the crossroads and follow a path which goes westwards from the crossroads then shortly south-westwards, shortly widening to become Church Lane; the views from Church Lane to the Uck valley and beyond are excellent, and make a good finale to your journey. Continue along Church Lane which in due course becomes Church Road. You're now back in Buxted and at the end of Church Road you reach the A272; turn right and walk a few yards to reach Buxted railway station which is to your right and from which regular trains are available from here to Uckfield, from which in turn there are buses back to Isfield.

One of the joys of riverside walking in Sussex is the variety of sights along the riverbanks. This is Shipley Windmill close to the infant river Adur.